The
QUEST
for
AUTHENTIC
POWER

The QUEST for
AUTHENTIC
POWER

Getting Past Manipulation,
Control, and Self-Limiting Beliefs

G. ROSS LAWFORD

BK

BERRETT-KOEHLER PUBLISHERS, INC.
San Francisco

Berrett-Koehler Publishers, Inc.
235 Montgomery Street, Suite 650
San Francisco, CA 94104-2916
Tel: (415) 288-0260   Fax: (415) 362-2512   www.bkconnection.com

ORDERING INFORMATION

Quantity sales. Special discounts are available on quantity purchases by corporations, associations, and others. For details, contact the "Special Sales Department" at the Berrett-Koehler address above.

Individual sales. Berrett-Koehler publications are available through most bookstores. They can also be ordered direct from Berrett-Koehler: Tel: (800) 929-2929; Fax: (802) 864-7626; www.bkconnection.com

Orders for college textbook/course adoption use. Please contact Berrett-Koehler: Tel: (800) 929-2929; Fax: (802) 864-7626.

Orders by U.S. trade bookstores and wholesalers. Please contact Publishers Group West, 1700 Fourth Street, Berkeley, CA 94710. Tel: (510) 528-1444; Fax: (510) 528-3444.

Berrett-Koehler and the BK logo are registered trademarks of Berrett-Koehler Publishers, Inc.

Printed in the United States of America

Berrett-Koehler books are printed on long-lasting acid-free paper. When it is available, we choose paper that has been manufactured by environmentally responsible processes. These may include using trees grown in sustainable forests, incorporating recycled paper, minimizing chlorine in bleaching, or recycling the energy produced at the paper mill.

Library of Congress Cataloging-in-Publication Data
Lawford, G. Ross, 1951–
   The quest for authentic power : getting past manipulation, control, and self-limiting beliefs / by G. Ross Lawford.
      p cm.
   Includes bibliographical references and index.
   ISBN 1-57675-147-3
   1. Leadership. 2. Power (Philosophy)   I. Title.
HD57.7.L378 2002
303.3—dc21   2002018376

Interior Design: Nancy Sabato
Project Management and Production: Shepherd, Inc.

FIRST EDITION

06 05 04 03 02   10 9 8 7 6 5 4 3 2 1

CONTENTS

PREFACE

In the beginning this book was simply a record of personal musings as I reflected on my own quest for authentic power. Later, as ideas and insights began to crystallize, I sought to test them against other people's experiences. Clients and others with whom I shared my thoughts and conclusions found them beneficial in their individual journeys and encouraged me to explore ways of making them available to as many people as possible. This publication is one result.

Certainly I know from first-hand experience how difficult it can be to get past manipulation and control, having grown up with a role model (father) who epitomized these strategies. In addition, my father fully exploited the prestige and status attached to having a Ph.D. in chemistry. It is only in retrospect, as I faced up to my own behavioral tendencies, that I could begin to understand the connections between my behavior, my father's behavior, and our common subconscious assumptions about the nature of power.

As an academic and a researcher, I had an opportunity to experience life within an extremely hierarchical organizational structure, which I realized later from my vantage point in business, was a fairly cut-throat environment. When I moved from academia to the business world, I personally experienced what it is like to have a boss who uses control and intimidation tactics, restricts access to information, uses "put downs," and opens other people's personal mail.

Later, as a business executive myself, first as divisional general manager in a very large corporation, and subsequently as president of a small company, I became dedicated to finding ways to manage effectively without resorting to manipulation and control. I had witnessed first-hand the many serious deficiencies of these strategies. I became convinced that there had to be a better way, not just to manage people, but to live all aspects of one's life. In the process of studying, reflecting upon and re-interpreting past experiences, and experimenting with new ideas and approaches, I began to realize how all these experiences were connected—*they were all influenced in some way by our concepts of power.*

In 1993 I devoted myself full-time to further exploring the subject of power. I was particularly intrigued by many different types of power, such as the power to heal, to reconcile, to facilitate, and to create. As I sought to understand the bases of these and other powers and experience them for myself, I was fortunate to have many wonderful teachers. At the same time I began a facilitation and coaching practice to assist individuals and organizations to be more effective in reaching their goals.

My understanding of power, particularly those things that limit our experience of authentic power, was further refined as I worked with my clients to help them move past limiting beliefs on the way to creating the kind of life and the kind of organizations they really wanted. A surprising number of the people I worked with, in spite of exhibiting all the outward signs of power and prosperity, confessed to feeling lonely, anxious, unfulfilled, empty, unhappy, discontent, or afraid. It has been a privilege for me to learn together with these clients how to get past the manipulation, control, and status-based strategies we grew up with, and to break through the self-limiting beliefs that have denied us the experience of authentic power. The transformation has often been dramatic.

Finally, this book has become more than a vehicle for making sense of my own quest for authentic power or a record of my personal struggle to get past my long-standing beliefs about power. It has become a collective work—a synthesis of wisdom derived from many sources. It has been influenced by the study of formal bodies of knowledge, a variety of cultural traditions, ancient wisdom, and the everyday experiences of many individuals. I find it difficult to adequately acknowledge all the contributors both because there were so many—teachers, authors, editors, friends, family, colleagues, and clients—and because I was often not even consciously aware of being influenced. I am especially grateful to my clients who so generously shared their own stories—both their successes and their setbacks—so that we could grow in wisdom together.

In offering this collected wisdom to you, the reader, I do so with the full conviction that, wherever you may be in your own journey, you will find, as many of my clients have, that it will facilitate your quest for authentic power in ways that will be life-transforming.

More Power to You!

Ross Lawford
Toronto, Canada
March 2002

Our Beliefs about Power Are Keeping Us Powerless

I n the final analysis, *power is about being able to transform your desires into a sustainable reality*. Most of us find we can't do that, and so we end up feeling relatively powerless. Instead of things going our way, things tend to go against us, and we get the impression we have to fight for every gain.

Having real power means setting as a goal something really important to us, and achieving that goal—not just for a while or just occasionally—but for as long as we want. For example, most of us want to have meaningful work—work that is neither dehumanizing nor bought at the expense of a balanced life. Most people also want to be part of relationships where they are loved or appreciated for themselves alone, not just because they meet someone else's needs and expectations.

When Disillusionment Happens

For a while we may cling to the illusion of being in control and being able to make things happen the way we want. Sooner or later, however, something happens to shatter our illusions. A crisis or a failure of some kind brings us face-to-face with the limitations of our power. We realize how impotent we actually are, especially when it comes to achieving the things that matter to us the most—loving relationships, joy, peace of mind, a sense of purpose, and a feeling of fulfillment.

Being forced to admit our inability to consistently achieve this quality of life for which we yearn is often a stimulus to try even harder. The beliefs on which these renewed efforts are based, however, usually remain unchallenged. Consequently, the results are again disappointing and the feelings of powerlessness intensify.

Even those of us who have succeeded in raising our standard of living have found that our quality of life—in terms of what is most important to us—has not improved in step with our standard of living as we expected. Instead stress levels are increasing dramatically and with them the incidence of stress-related health problems. Burnout, depression, frustration, and loneliness are more and more prevalent.

All the labor-saving and time-saving devices that modern technology has given us have not produced for us the outcomes we most deeply desire. Underneath the veneer of success and prosperity is an enduring emptiness—a longing that we seem powerless to satisfy. We remain convinced that there must be something more to life, if only we knew where and how to find it.

In our search for that "something more," we turn increasingly to self-help books and experts of all types, desperately trying the latest techniques that promise to make us better managers, better parents, better lovers, or better investors. We experiment with new diets, join fitness programs, pay out money for alternative approaches to health, and seek new ways of becoming more spiritual. I have no quarrel with any of these approaches, but I do question their ability to bring about the desired outcomes if they are used in conjunction with the same old belief systems, particularly the commonly-held beliefs about power. In fact, experience shows that after a brief honeymoon period, these new approaches tend to be abandoned in favor of the next fad as we find ourselves pretty well back where we started—feeling disappointed, discouraged, and powerless.

The Path to Self-Empowerment

The conclusions on which this book is based are.

* ✱ *It is our beliefs about power—many of them subconscious beliefs—that are keeping us powerless.*
* ✱ *Becoming genuinely more powerful means changing those beliefs.*

The emphasis of this book is on freeing you from reliance on those invalid, subconscious beliefs that keep you powerless. The alternatives presented will help you to connect with a source of authentic power. They will make you effective at realizing your desired outcomes—whether these be specific goals, such as closing a sale or being more assertive, or quality of life goals, such as achieving peace of mind.

Key to this self-empowerment process is *learning to see old things in new ways* as opposed to concentrating on *new* approaches, techniques, or recipes. This book will equip you with these new ways of looking at power.

* You will understand why the strategies and specific techniques you have used in the past have been ineffective or inappropriate.
* You will understand why, in spite of your good intentions, you have so often failed to produce the outcomes you desired.
* You will be shown the way to unleash the amazing power of those intentions.

- You will learn to rely on your own wisdom to answer each question as it arises based on the specifics of the particular situation instead of depending on prescribed answers. You will know, for example, when to stand fast and when to stand aside, in which situations to establish boundaries and what boundaries are most appropriate, or what amount of accountability is called for and what form would be most effective.

The process of getting past your self-limiting beliefs about the nature of power begins with an increased understanding of those beliefs and the possibilities to be realized by adopting a new paradigm. Toward this end, the book will ask basic questions about the nature of power. Answers provided by the conventional viewpoint will be contrasted with the answers that emerge when power is viewed in a new way. Because the power described by this new paradigm is so much more effective at transforming our desires into sustainable reality, I refer to it as *authentic power.*

This power is also authentic because it comes from adherence to your principles and values—not the principles and values you espouse because they are expedient or because you think you should, but the ones deep at the heart of your being, i.e., the ones that derive from your authentic Self. This book will help you with the difficult task of uncovering your authentic Self and in so doing put you on the road to finding *authentic power.*

The following table acts as a road map for your journey. It provides an overview of the concepts in the book and how these concepts relate to each other. You may find it helpful to review this table occasionally as you proceed through the book.

THE DIMENSIONS OF POWER

What is power?

A CONVENTIONAL VIEW OF POWER	WHAT IS AUTHENTIC POWER?
1. Power as authority	1. Power as authenticity
2. Power as control	2. Power as synergy
3. Power as strength	3. Power as inner strength
4. Power as status	4. Power as "quality of being"

How is power obtained?

ASSUMPTIONS OF THE CONVENTIONAL PARADIGM	THE PARADIGM OF AUTHENTIC POWER
1. Power as a commodity	1. The power of intention
2. Power as a reward	2. The authentic Self as the source

What limits our power?

ASSUMPTIONS OF THE CONVENTIONAL PARADIGM	THE PARADIGM OF AUTHENTIC POWER
1. Other people and circumstances	1. Our own beliefs
	2. Unconsciousness

How is power exercised?

STRATEGIES OF THE CONVENTIONAL PARADIGM	STRATEGIES FOR EXERCISING AUTHENTIC POWER
1. The "control strategy"	1. Empower yourself
2. The "bulldozer strategy"	2. Create an empowering environment
3. One-upmanship	3. Build synergy ("power with")

CHAPTER 1

Our Concepts of Power Shape Our Reality

For many people the quest for power is all consuming, and why not? No other concept has as much influence in shaping our lives as power does. Power, not love as the song suggests, is what "makes the world go round." With enough power, most of us believe, you can do anything, achieve any goal, and be in control of every situation. However, when it comes to fundamental questions about the nature of power—how to achieve and maintain power and how to exercise power effectively—most of us would have to admit to not ever having consciously considered these matters. Instead, we allow unquestioned, subconscious assumptions about power to direct our every move.

Make no mistake about it, however, our understanding—conscious or unconscious—of what power is and how to use it shows up in how we relate to employees, supervisors, and colleagues. Just as surely it determines how we relate to spouses, parents, children, and friends. Indeed the nature of every relationship we have, whether to people, things, or the environment, is determined in large measure by our concepts of power. This being the case, surely it would behoove us to examine our understanding of power and how it works, to separate the myths from the reality, and to learn how to be truly effective through the use of *authentic* power.

Uncovering Some of Our Assumptions about Power

The first thing we all do in any situation is to size up where the power lies. This process involves both perception and interpretation. It happens so automatically that usually we are not even aware that we are doing it. In making this assessment of the relative power of the players, we use many different kinds of clues, such as body language, manner of dress, degree of self-confidence, apparent popularity, how articulate the person is, his or her title, etc. The person sitting at the head of the table, the person facing the door, and a person behind a desk are usually assumed to be powerful relative to others in the room.

Being somewhat short in stature myself, I notice that I automatically feel a little intimidated in the presence of tall people, particularly men. It's more comfortable for me to be standing while others sit because that way I feel taller. This may also explain why I feel comfortable standing in front of an audience. I'm told that some managers stand behind their desks and have the person they are about to fire or reprimand sit in front of them as a way of emphasizing the power differential between them.

My purpose in mentioning these examples is to point out that such intimidation techniques are only effective when used with people whose automatic interpretation of greater height is that it means greater power. Most people share the same assumptions and beliefs about power and, therefore, most of society behaves in predictable ways. Also these beliefs become accepted as the only possible way of interpreting situations in life. This holds true even if the beliefs themselves are neither rational nor consistent with actual experience.

Actually, equating height and power is a rather silly assumption even if it perhaps made sense at a more primitive stage in our evolution. You can probably think of exceptions in your own experience where powerful people were short. Come to think of it, the other assumptions that we automatically use to assess the relative power of people might not be any more valid than the height one. In most cases we are not even consciously aware of most of the criteria we are using.

Here is a way for you to uncover some of your personal assumptions about power. Quickly assign one of the following categories to each person on the list below:

1. Very powerful
2. Powerful
3. Slightly powerful
4. Fairly powerless
5. Quite powerless

chair of the board
doctor
homemaker
professor
president or prime
    minister of a country
the queen
student
the mayor of a city
minister or priest or rabbi
a general in the armed forces
law enforcement officer
movie star
homeless person

supervisor
chief financial officer
partner in a law firm
social worker
nurse
assembly line worker
retired dentist
garbage collector
yourself
member of congress or
    parliament
mental patient
female receptionist
bank vice president

Now look back at your rankings and consider these questions:

- What specifically was it about those you rated as "very powerful" or "powerful" that caused you to assign that particular rating?
- What specifically was lacking in those you rated as "fairly powerless" or "quite powerless?"
- How did you rank yourself? Why?
- What personal assumptions about power have you uncovered?

Each of us will rank the individuals in the list differently. Nevertheless we all have perceptions about power that influence our judgments of others. That is, we have preconceived notions of power relative to such criteria as knowledge, age, gender, physical strength, and popularity. We also tend to use more than one criterion at a time. You might have wondered, for example, if the law enforcement officer is male or female, if the professor is tenured, or if the retired dentist is wealthy. But by using one criterion to describe each of the people, I hope I've helped to bring your preconceptions more to the forefront. Realize that *your judgments affect how you treat others*; for example, society places more value on wealthy people and marginalizes the poor.

✳ *An Opportunity for Personal Reflection* ✳

How might your preconceived notions about power be affecting your interactions with the people around you?
Of whom are you most critical? Most intolerant? Why?
By whom are you most intimidated? Why?
Around whom do you feel inferior? Why?

If our assumptions are not really valid indicators of power, or if we misread the situation for any other reason, then our subsequent behavior is likely to be ineffective, or worse still, inappropriate. If, for example, in a business meeting, I misread the clues based on incorrect assumptions, I might conclude that I am at a power disadvantage. Unless I am very good at bluffing, my body language, tone of voice, and general attitude will all betray how I feel and make me indeed appear weak and ineffectual. Alternatively I might overcompensate for feeling like the underdog and come across with unnecessary aggression. Surely there is a more accurate way to measure power than the subconscious assumptions on which most of us presently rely. Having studied this matter, I am convinced that *by changing our assumptions about power, we can not only gain a more accurate measure of power but also gain access to a more effective and a more authentic power.*

The Way We Use the Word *Power*

In Andrew Lloyd Weber's rock musical *Jesus Christ Superstar* (lyrics by Tim Rice), Jesus tells Simon, "Neither you, Simon, nor the fifty thousand . . . understand what power is . . . understand at all." I've become convinced that we probably haven't progressed much in our understanding of power compared to the people of two thousand years ago. One place our confusion about power shows up is in our language. We may understand the centrality of power in our lives, what with everything from power plays in hockey to power lunches, power naps, power windows, power struggles, and balance of power. When it comes to speaking about power, however, our language exposes the vagueness of our understanding.

Given that the concept of power is so crucial to the way we live our lives, you might be justified in thinking that the concept of power would have evolved to a high degree, and that the word *power* would have a fairly concise and universal meaning. You might reasonably expect that the word *power* would evoke the same understanding for everyone and in every circumstance. The fact that this is not the case is part of the problem. Have you ever noticed how many different meanings are subsumed by the one word *power?* The way we use the word power reminds me of the loose way we use the word *love* to mean everything from lust, to a selfless caring for someone. We can speak of *loving* football, our parents, someone to whom we are sexually attracted, and God—all in one breath. In the same way we speak of *power* when we refer to electricity, physical strength, authority, influence, charisma, control, and a host of other attributes.

Webster's New Explorer Dictionary (1999) gives several different meanings for the word *power.* One set of meanings concerns *the ability to act or produce an effect.* In other cases, power refers to *a position of ascendancy over others.* Another group of meanings relates to *control and authority.* Power is also used to mean *physical might.* In physics, power is a measure of *the rate at which work is done or energy transferred.*

Multiple Meanings Add to the Confusion

The use of one word to convey such different meanings creates problems for us. For example the kind of power that one has by virtue of having a certain position is quite different from inter-personal power, i.e., the power that people cede to you because you have "people talent"—the ability to establish rapport with others, to understand their needs, and the willingness to try to meet those needs.

Because we use the same word for all the different meanings of the word *power,* we tend to transfer our assumptions about one kind of power to the others as if these properties applied equally to all kinds of power. This can be illustrated with the usage of power to mean *authority,* as in *power of attorney.* This kind of power can clearly be transferred; that is, it can be given by one person to another. I could *authorize* you to look after my financial affairs or, in a similar vein, I *authorize* an elected person to represent my interests in the governing of the country.

This kind of power comes with a particular position. When you think about it, though, you will realize that this "positional power" is more about *responsibility* than it is about the ability to get something done.

The power to get results is quite different; it cannot be transferred from one person to another. Knowledge can be transferred, but how can I possibly give you my ability to achieve intended results? Underlying our thinking about power, however, is the hidden assumption that *all* kinds of power are transferable from one person to another, i.e., that one person can *empower* another. From this assumption it is only a small step to the assumption that, if someone else has more power or if I am feeling relatively powerless, then I need some of the other person's power. The inevitable result is a "power struggle."

My response to this confusion is to try to separate some of the different meanings of the word *power* in normal usage and to make more explicit the assumptions around each separate meaning. As these assumptions are subjected to conscious scrutiny, I think you will find that most of them are invalid, or at least misleading—certainly not worthy of the place in our lives that they presently occupy. Since the conventional view of power is proving to be so inadequate, it would seem all the more important to begin exploring alternative, more helpful paradigms. I will refer to the power represented by these new concepts as *authentic power*.

How Did We Arrive at These Beliefs about Power?

From a very early age each of us has been trying to answer fundamental questions such as "Who am I?" and "How can I get what I want?" As children we formed answers to these questions by interpreting our experiences and the messages we received from significant people around us. Many of the messages we received were confusing—even contradictory. Nevertheless, we formed conclusions and internalized them—largely in the form of subconscious beliefs. We noticed that in many respects we seemed powerless; that control and getting our way went with being more grown up, stronger, and smarter. We noticed that affirmation and attention came more readily when we met certain criteria set by those in control. This is the process by which we formed our beliefs about power. Not surprisingly, those beliefs are similar to the (subconscious) beliefs held by our parents.

If our present beliefs and assumptions about power are so questionable, why have they persisted, largely unexamined, into our adult lives? Part of the answer is undoubtedly that having been held virtually unchallenged for so long, these assumptions have graduated to become part of our core belief system. Core beliefs are assumptions that we *assume* are facts. This kind of reinforcing of assumptions by experience is a natural consequence of how our perception-interpretation process works.

> **Perception:** Any perceptions that do not fit with already-held beliefs and assumptions tend to be filtered out before they even reach our consciousness. We simply see and hear what we expect to see and hear.

> **Interpretation:** Even if a discrepancy manages to get through this first filter, like all perceptions it still needs to be interpreted—"What is this I'm seeing or hearing?" Perceptions that don't fit the pre-existing mental model or that can't be explained by it are often dismissed as spurious or the result of inaccurate perception.

This perception-interpretation process easily precludes changes in attitudes and beliefs—except in the case of determined, conscious effort—and pretty well assures that whatever illusions I have I will continue to experience as real.

We don't often realize, however, that *our beliefs and assumptions are shaping our reality.* Daniel Kim (*The Systems Thinker,*

Vol. 4, No. 2, 1993) gives this example: Suppose that all of us in the office had concluded that Bob doesn't really care about meetings and is not a team player. What would we begin to notice about Bob? We would take note of all the times he shows up late, and we would probably ignore, or not even be aware of, all the times he is on time. We would notice that Bob does not say much at meetings, but fail to register the fact that a few people always dominate the conversation and that there are others who say even less than Bob. In other words we would continually filter out any information that doesn't fit in with the mental model we have created about Bob. In fact all the data we see confirm our beliefs and assumptions about Bob.

This example shows that groups or corporations may develop a shared belief system about reality by the same process as individuals. The only hope of discovering or adopting new, more valid beliefs rests in by-passing this process. Organizations that have figured out how to do this are referred to as *Learning Organizations* by Peter Senge of MIT's Sloan School of Management. Our prevailing beliefs about power are keeping us, as individuals and as organizations, locked in the *illusion* of power and therefore unable to experience *authentic* power.

✴ An Opportunity for Personal Reflection ✴

People's preconceived ideas limited their experience of Bob. What adjectives or labels do you use to characterize particular neighbors and coworkers?

Try to think of these people using very different words to describe each of them.

Notice how difficult it is for you to let go of your previous opinions. As you try to imagine them in new terms, do you find yourself trying to defend your original impressions?

Your Power May Be Counterfeit

I have already noted how central is the role of power in our lives. It is so central that power could well be considered the universal currency for every transaction in life. On the other hand, I have noted that the assumptions by which we define and assess power are highly suspect. We are left to ponder questions such as these:

"Might our 'currency' actually be counterfeit?"

"Could our quest for power turn out to be little more than a fantasy?"

"How can we know whether our prevailing concepts of power are truly authentic or only a counterfeit version of the real thing?"

Surely the acid test is whether or not power, as we know it, is *able to translate intention into reality in a sustainable fashion.* This is the definition of power that I will use throughout the book. Based on this criterion, however, most of what traditionally goes by the name *power* comes up short.

One reason that these shortcomings are not more obvious is that we are often not very clear in our own minds about our intentions. If our intentions are confused, then we will be less likely to notice that they have not been realized. Regardless of the strategy being employed or the immediate goals identified, what everyone I've talked to really wants are things that traditional approaches to power and the resulting facsimiles of power simply cannot deliver, namely peace of mind, a feeling of self-worth, and to feel loved. The things for which they strive so terribly hard—standard of living, achievement, success, fame, lifestyle, excitement—are simply assumed to be gateways to happiness and fulfillment, peace of mind, etc.

While strategies based on prevailing ideas about power may appear to work, they really don't. You can't achieve peace of mind or love using control strategies any more than you can buy these deep feelings. Sometimes we succumb to the illusion that we can buy or demand loyalty or love or respect. But, just as a big difference exists between buying sex from a prostitute and making love, a great qualitative difference exists between the loyalty from an employee's heart and the loyalty gotten from an employee by a raise or a threat.

Actually one needn't look only at ultimate outcomes to notice that strategies based on force and control are not usually effective in accomplishing even everyday goals like getting the most from employees or persuading children to do what you want them to do. The reason is that there are limits to what can reasonably be controlled. A boss can't possibly watch over every employee, just as it is impossible for parents to watch their children's every move. Eventually it becomes necessary to use force or some other form of intimidation to maintain control, however, you must be willing and able to use force and to make good on the threats. If not, your bluff may be called and you will lose control. This kind of thinking is used to justify everything from an arms race to labor strikes to spanking children. If you do use these techniques to force your will on others or to maintain control over them, however, you risk winning the battle and losing the war—hardly what you would call a demonstration of real power!

Typical Responses to Feelings of Powerlessness

Unfortunately many people blame themselves instead of their concepts of power when they are unable to realize their goals. They don't stop to question their strategy or the premise on which it is based; they assume that their ineffectiveness and apparent powerlessness are because they are not trying hard enough. Instead of changing to a more effective strategy, most people, when facing an inability to convert intention into reality, fall back on that old maxim, "If at first you don't succeed, try, try again." Trying harder while clinging to an incorrect premise, is simply a recipe for stress and burnout. It cannot turn a bad plan into a good one. No wonder so many people live lives of desperate striving, frustrated burnout, depression, or angry resignation!

In this vulnerable, stressed condition, it's easy to be further seduced into thinking that the solution lies in hiring the right people, wearing the "in" fashions, drinking the right beer, finding the right mate, belonging to the right clubs, going to the right schools, driving the coolest car, associating with the most powerful people, choosing the right career, having the right body shape, behaving in "acceptable" ways, . . . the list of *shoulds* and *oughts* goes on and on.

Faced with the ineffectiveness of the kind of power that we've spent our life's energy pursuing, it's customary to conclude not only that we need to try harder but also that we need *more power*. If a little isn't effective, we reason, maybe more will do the trick. Thus the natural response to feeling relatively powerless in any situation seems to be to further intensify the quest for power until the quest becomes an addiction. The sad fact is, as with any addiction, more is never enough. It takes more and more to feed the habit—more affluence, more control, more affirmations, more conquests, etc. Come to think of it, maybe all the common addictions—whether to gambling, to shopping, to sex, to drugs, or to work—are all just specific forms of our addiction to the quest for power.

In our quest for power and what we imagine it will bring us, *we actually end up allowing other things and other people to control our lives*. This control takes several forms. It can be as subtle as a belief about how we *should* or *ought* to behave, and it can be as blatant as an all-consuming drive to achieve something. Even when it appears to be strictly our own agenda that we are following, the underlying beliefs that cause our behavior have come from someone else. Strategies based on these beliefs don't actually make us more powerful, although often we cling to that illusion. Instead these strategies cause us to become mere "oughtomatons," or robots, unwittingly buying into someone else's method of controlling our behavior. "Be perfect, work hard, be humble, be clean, be obedient, be a good student, be attractive, don't rock the boat, be strong, don't show your emotions," say the voices in our heads.

These strategies and the subconscious beliefs on which they are based make us harder workers, more compliant employees, citizens, spouses, or children; they also make us insatiable consumers of whatever other people suggest we *should* have. Because they are based on incorrect, rarely challenged assumptions, however, these strategies ultimately end in failure and frustration. *The natural result of being addicted to the quest for this kind of power is actually an increasing feeling of powerlessness.*

✳ *An Opportunity for Personal Reflection* ✳

In what specific ways is your life controlled by the expectations and brainwashing of others—parents (even though you are an adult), bosses, advertisers, significant others, community, etc.?
How important are social pressures in determining your behavior?
Why do you let yourself be controlled by others?
Has trying to meet all these expectations brought you the quality of life you really want?

Not everyone who realizes the ineffectiveness of his or her strategies does so gradually. For an increasing number of people, it comes as a major wake-up call. Unfortunately, the wake-up call frequently takes the form of a job loss, bankruptcy, or marriage breakdown; sometimes all of these happen at once. This kind of jolt is no longer reserved for mid-life, middle-management types. As the dot-com economy flounders, for example, many people in their twenties who thought they had a lot of power are finding themselves with nothing. All too frequently people experience these events as a personal crisis and fall into emotional instability, depression, or substance abuse. In crisis mode, however, it's easy to miss the opportunity that's being presented to examine one's root assumptions about power and to replace them with more empowering ones.

If power is *the ability to translate intention into reality on a sustainable basis* what these people are experiencing is a profound sense of powerlessness whether they would use that word or not. Of course the realization that the notions of power that have shaped one's life are misguided at best, and more likely bankrupt, can happen at any time of life; it can happen at a vaguely conscious or totally subconscious level. Often events take place that force us to admit to ourselves that things are just not working. Blame may arbitrarily be laid on the doorstep of parents, the boss, the economy, the spouse, bad luck, or almost anything.

Finding someone or something to blame takes the focus away from the real issues; consequently people in crisis, mid-life or otherwise, tend to make changes indiscriminately—new corporate policy, new management personnel, new organizational structure, new spouse, new car (house, job, location, etc.). Unfortunately, these random changes produce no more effective results than before because the key underlying assumptions remain the same.

To Change Your Outcomes, Change Your Assumptions

As in all complex systems with many interacting components, there are several points at which interventions may be made in order to change to a more effective or desirable outcome. In the matter of achieving a more authentic, and therefore more satisfying experience of personal power, as in most other matters, the obvious interventions tend to be the least effective. This is why the usual tactics—trying harder or changing partners, jobs, structures, etc.—rarely produce lasting gains of the type desired.

The main point of leverage for becoming more effective in translating intentions into reality in a way that is sustainable is to alter the beliefs and assumptions about power that are at the very heart of the systems within which we operate. In fact, so fundamental are our beliefs about power that to alter them is to change virtually every aspect of our lives. Change our assumptions about power, and we will change how we educate, how we govern, how we deliver health care, how we administer justice, how we respond to authority, how we relate to the environment—indeed how we relate to everyone and how we respond to every circumstance and situation.

The old assumptions function to keep us constantly insecure, anxious, needy, and therefore, relatively powerless. Are we irrevocably locked into these patterns? Must we continue for the rest of our lives controlled by subconscious beliefs and assumptions, and therefore denied the experience of authentic power? I don't think so, but breaking free of this pattern that holds us so firmly in its grip will require considerable conscious effort. The habitual attitudes and behaviors of a lifetime are not easily dismissed.

One way of thinking about the kind of conscious effort required to break free of these old patterns is provided by the following exercise, which I have used several times with groups. People are handed cards cut in specific shapes. As each new shape is presented, the recipient is instructed to arrange all the shapes in their possession at that point to form a rectangle. The second and third shapes can easily be added to the first, in each case forming a bigger rectangle. However, the fourth shape simply cannot be added to the existing rectangle to form a bigger one. This is as far as most people get because they try to do with the fourth card what worked with the other cards. The only way one can proceed to form a rectangle is to scramble the card shapes and then to start again to assemble them in an entirely new way. The pattern of beliefs and assumptions that make up our world view are like those shapes. After a certain point in our lives, the only way to make sense of things anymore is to *scramble the shapes and rearrange them*, so to speak.

Examining our core beliefs about power can be very frightening because it could turn our whole world upside down; it could even threaten our image of who we are. Although it is less threatening, it is also less effective to keep on tinkering with the various aspects of our life separately—restructuring the workplace, rewriting the policy manual, changing the political party in office, firing the team coach, getting a facelift or a new wardrobe, and so on. My grandfather used to characterize these approaches as "changing robbers in the middle of a hold-up." They could also be compared to trying different techniques to remove the pollution from a waterway without first going upstream to the source of the pollution and stopping it.

Efforts to modify behavior, whether as individuals, communities or organizations, will continue to result in relapse until we go "upstream" and modify the belief system that is giving rise to that particular behavior in the first place. You may have experienced this if you have lived through an organizational restructuring, or on a personal level if you have tried unsuccessfully to lose weight or quit smoking. On the other hand, if the assumptions and beliefs behind the ineffective or undesirable habitual behavior can be made explicit and then modified, hitherto unreachable outcomes can be achieved almost effortlessly. The secret to success in the quest for authentic power lies in realizing that your experience of powerlessness is largely a result of the beliefs and assumptions you hold and then abandoning those beliefs in favor of more empowering ones.

CHAPTER

A Conventional
View of Power

I f our beliefs and assumptions about the nature of power are
keeping us powerless, then surely it is important to develop a
better understanding of these limiting beliefs. In answering the
question, "What is power?," the conventional view is usually
expressed in terms of authority, control, strength, and status. Let's
begin by examining each of these kinds of power more closely.

Power as Authority

✳ *An Opportunity for Personal Reflection* ✳

*Think of specific people whom you regard as having "authority." Do
you think of these people as having power?*
If so, what specific power does each of these people have?
What is it that gives them this power?

The power of authority is really *power by virtue of position*. This
is the so-called power of the foreman over the line worker, the

manager over the foreman, the vice president over the manager, and the president over the vice president. It is also the power we assume that parents have over children, doctors have over patients, and police have over citizens. The amount of power one has is assumed to increase the higher the person's position in some hierarchical relationship. What generally does increase as one progresses up in a hierarchical system, is the amount of authority granted to that person. Because we tend to equate authority with power, we naturally speak of people who have more authority as having more power.

Historically, monarchs have claimed this "position power" as a "divine right." As a consequence, monarchs of questionable sanity and competence have ruled entire nations on no other basis than the authority that came with a position or title. Even today this principle continues to operate in the workplace. For example, my friend's boss thinks that his position in the hierarchy gives him the right to make ill-considered commands, yell, badger, intimidate, and generally treat his employees with contempt. Consider also how many employees regard their bosses as complete incompetents. No doubt this accounts for the popularity of the *Dilbert* cartoon series.

Authority is really quite different from the ability to make things happen, as anyone has quickly discovered who has tried to get something done on the basis of authority alone. Employees, for example, may or may not *choose* to facilitate the wishes and expectations of their bosses. When they choose, for whatever reason, to act in accordance with the boss' wishes, they may make their boss *appear* powerful. However it is important to realize that *the power to choose is stronger than the so-called power of authority*—the boss' position, in and of itself, does not give the boss the power or the ability to dictate that choice.

The authority-power relationship between management and employees is not that much different than that between parents and children.

"Stop doing that," you tell your little child.

"Why?" is the response.

"Because Mommy says so," you reply evoking the authority of your position as parent.

Honestly, though, for how long is "pulling rank" on your child really effective? When the child is really intent on doing what he is doing, and particularly when that child becomes a teenager, isn't the response likely to be the challenge, "Make me?" Of course, you know full well that you can't make him and that only makes you angry.

The truth is that *we can't make a child, an employee, or anyone for that matter, do something if they choose not to.* Oh we can (and often do, in such circumstances) resort to force or threat to get our own way, however, we shouldn't confuse the power of authority with the power of coercion or intimidation.

Often as parents and managers we succumb to using our authority as the basis for threats and coercion. This can be a dangerous game to play as someone I know discovered one day when he tried to discipline his son by *making* him go upstairs to his bedroom. The boy had grown too big to be simply picked up and carried up the stairs, but in trying to push him up the stairs, his father failed to realize just how big he had become—that is until the boy turned around and punched him so hard that it knocked the wind out of him. So much for the power of parental authority! Yet in attempting to exercise authority, as we call it, over children, employees, or anyone, *what we are really teaching them is that the person, who by virtue of his or her position, can make the biggest threat, has the most power.* Is it any surprise then, that:

- Employees who feel relatively powerless join unions?
- Children who feel relatively powerless become delinquents?
- Fearful citizens become vigilantes?

If the authority that comes with having a responsible position in the hierarchical structure of an organization does not necessarily mean having power, what does it mean? Surely the answer to this question is contained in the question itself. Surely what comes with a responsible position is *responsibility*. Saying that the boss has a responsibility to shareholders and employees, however, is quite different from saying that the boss, by virtue of his or her position, has the power to make things happen. In other words, the power of the parent and the boss is not really power at all; it is authority granted by someone else to take care of someone or something. It is a *responsibility!* The person to whom a *power of attorney* is granted, has a *responsibility* to act on behalf of someone else. The same meaning can be attached to the power of elected members of the government. The electorate has given them a *responsibility* to govern and to make decisions on their behalf.

Yet how often do we behave as if people in positions of authority have power over us? How often do we see ourselves as powerless in front of them? This is not to suggest that bosses and parents and big brothers and all sorts of people don't try to use threats to make us do what they want us to. Bosses may remind us that they can fire us; parents may threaten to ground us; and big brother says he'll beat us up. Intimidation tactics of this type are not new; they were included in the advice given by Machiavelli in 1513 in the document known as *The Prince*. Machiavelli believed that people could not be controlled and directed without the application of force and at least the threat of violence. This kind of thinking once formed the basis for what was considered effective leadership. Not all people in positions of authority today resort to these strong-arm tactics, but many still do. Intimidation, however, is not a truly effective way of discharging responsibility. What intimidation actually does is add to the feeling of powerlessness that many people feel.

It is probably true that the feeling of powerlessness that is shared by many workers is the single greatest cause of poor productivity in the workplace today. The problem might not be identified as a feeling of powerlessness; it might be given different names, such as low morale, high absenteeism, health problems, lack of commitment, laziness, or alcoholism. The solution, some think, is to empower the workers. Empowered workers should make for a more competitive enterprise, they reason. However, if power is the ability to achieve intended results, we have already seen that managers don't have that kind of power, at least not by virtue of their position.

The very word *empowerment* is problematic because it seems to say to the worker, "I have power and you don't; I will give you a little of mine so you can work more effectively." It doesn't surprise me that most empowerment programs fail to deliver the desired results. As a worker, I don't think I would be terribly motivated by such sharing of responsibility on the part of the boss (unless, of course, he proposed to share his salary in the same proportion). What is really happening in this situation is that the boss, who probably doesn't have any real power in the first place, is trying to motivate me by giving me, not the ability to do my job more effectively, but some of his authority/responsibility. This is simply a disguised form of delegation, not empowerment.

It is also true however, that some people in positions of authority demonstrate power in the sense that they do have the capacity to translate intention into reality, and they do it with the cooperation of the people around them. An example might be the parents who seem to have "ideal children" because they usually do what their parents ask without being threatened. It could be the boss whose loyal staff appear to bend over backwards to please, but not because of the performance bonus or the threat of being fired in the event of non-performance. If we examine these situations we will see that it is not their position that gives these people the apparent power to accomplish their agenda, but rather the people around them who have freely *chosen* to support this result by their actions.

Power as Control

Most often when we use the word *power*, we have in mind the idea of controlling the actions of someone or something. For instance, when we speak of being able to control our own behavior, we speak of having *will power*. We tend to automatically attribute to people in positions of authority the right as well as the ability to control the actions of others, and thereby produce the outcomes they desire. Yet, as we have already seen, this kind of power does not automatically accompany the authority vested in a position. It may appear that someone is controlling others by virtue of their position, but often the behavior is being influenced more by threats (be they implicit or explicit). Lawmakers have the power (authority) to set speed limits. The police have the power (authority) to enforce the speed limit. But even the force of their combined powers is not enough to control everyone's driving speed. Of course if you add the threat of fines or license suspension, the driving behavior of some individuals may be curtailed. Nevertheless not all drivers will make this choice; some will choose to drive within the limit only when there is a reasonable chance of getting caught for speeding, while others will drive as they please regardless.

In George Orwell's novel *Nineteen Eighty-Four* Winston Smith in considering the control-based society in which he lives, comes to a similar realization. He says "They can make you say anything but they can't make you believe it. . . ." What can we conclude then about the power to control? Is it perhaps only an illusion?

✳ *An Opportunity for Personal Reflection* ✳

Who do you try to control and what methods do you use?

Do you try to control others because you believe it is your right or because you believe it is your duty?

What does it feel like to lose control of a situation?

How does it feel when you perceive that someone is trying to control or manipulate you?

Power as Strength

Frequently, we mean *strength* when we use the word *power*. It is not uncommon, for example, to refer to a physically strong person as powerful. Similarly, we might call a nation powerful based on its military strength. Why not? People or countries that possess "strength of arms," whether literal arms or armaments, can usually get their own way. In other words the power to get something done is attributed to the person, group, or country perceived to have the highest capability to inflict pain or harm. The resulting intimidation is used to dominate or control the actions of others such that they accomplish what the so-called "powerful person" desires that they should accomplish. There it is—what we dignify with the name of power is, at its core, bullying and intimidation. Look around and you will see manipulation by intimidation masquerading as real power in every sphere of life— none is immune.

A Domination Hierarchy

Underlying the prevalent use of threat and intimidation is the belief that the persons with the most power are the ones most capable of carrying out their threats—the ones most capable of generating fear. This is the thinking not only behind the arms race and the schoolyard bully; it is also the basis of the power of parents, bosses, and police. The pain doesn't have to be physical; it can work just as well (maybe better) if it is emotional. This is the same method used by abusers of all types to maintain control and hence *feel* more powerful.

Nor does the intimidation need to be overt. In today's world it is frequently subtle, as in the feeling a girl gets that the boy won't "like" her anymore if she doesn't give in to his sexual or other demands. It's as subtle as knowing that your job is always on the line and that you could lose it simply by failing to volunteer for extra duty. Nobody needs to say these things, but you feel powerless because you know that the person in a position of power has the ability to cause you harm. Isn't that how one wins a power struggle?—by finding some way to inflict more harm than your opponent, or perhaps by getting something that can be held over the opponent's head?

This way of viewing power naturally leads to yet another type of hierarchy—the *domination hierarchy*—based on the extent of one's capability to cause pain or harm. Indeed, maybe all other hierarchies are simply subsets of this domination one! This may be fairly obvious if we are considering a hierarchy of nations based on military might. If we look carefully, however, we can glimpse the same principle behind corporate and other organizational hierarchies. Maybe that explains why people in "matrix" or other "organic" organizational structures often feel uncomfortable. "Who's the boss?" they want to know. Because they don't know exactly of whom to be afraid, they fear everybody. There are even less obvious hierarchies, for example the one deep in the psyches of most of us—the one that places males above females. How about the one that puts the poor at the mercy of the wealthy, the disabled behind the able-bodied, or makes the under-schooled feel inferior in the presence of the highly educated?

Maintaining a Dominant Position

One of the consequences of achieving power status based on domination is that eventually the capability to inflict harm will have to be demonstrated if the power status is to remain credible. Sooner or later your claim to power will be challenged by a pretender to your "throne." The inevitable result of this form of power is abuse and often violence!

If you doubt the overwhelming acceptance of this view of power in our society, notice the prevalence of militaristic and pugnacious language in all aspects of our everyday life. We go to work to "do battle." We "fight" for a promotion or a parking place. Political or business rivals are "the enemy." Our approach to our competitors is to "knock 'em dead!" We encourage persistence by saying "stick to your guns." Doctors speak of "declaring war" on cancer. One political candidate "defeats" another in an election. Marketers consider whether their "war chest" is big enough to sustain a "price war," and these discussions may take place in their "war room." People or organizations sustaining a "barrage" of criticism might be described as being "under attack" or "embattled." Even jokes have to have a "punch" line. You may be thinking that this is inconsequential—that these are simply harmless expressions. But these expressions provide evidence of our subconscious belief that power is demonstrated by domination; at the same time these expressions reinforce those very beliefs every time we repeat them.

✳ An Opportunity for Personal Reflection ✳

How many other examples can you add to the list of militaristic language in everyday life?

One of the consequences of using this type of language is that it causes us to think of people, diseases, and organizations as "the enemy." Who and what are the enemies in your life?

In what ways does this kind of thinking turn your life into a struggle or a battle?

The belief that power means having domination over someone or something is not only very old, it is also quite entrenched in our psyches. Referring to it as the "domination system," Walter Wink in *Engaging the Powers* traces the idea back to an ancient Babylonian myth. A power struggle and a murder are the very bases of creation in this story.

Escaping from the Domination Approach

Riane Eisler has also written extensively about what she calls "the dominator model" in her two books: *The Chalice and the Blade* and *Sacred Pleasure*. In the second of these books she looks far back in history to a time before sex became a means of domination, a time before sexual violence and "the war of the sexes" became commonplace. In so doing, she lifts up hope that we can create for ourselves and our children new ways of living together based on new assumptions. She calls this alternative way of thinking "the partnership model." It's not really new; other societies, even some animals, have been known to exhibit this kind of cooperative behavior. A change in our present way of viewing power is of immediate urgency, though, because as she puts it:

> . . . ours is a time when man's conquest of nature threatens all life on our planet, when a dominator mindset and advanced technology are a potentially lethal mix, when all around us institutions designed to maintain domination and exploitation are proving incapable of coping with the massive social, economic, and ecological problems they have created. (*Sacred Pleasure*)

It's hard to escape the assumptions of the dominator model. For example our TV and movie heroes glorify the concept that "might is right" and that violence, in any proportion, is an appropriate way to achieve one's goals. This, then, is the belief system that we teach our children from the time they are old enough to watch cartoons. Actually, westerns, cop shows, and spy thrillers share basically the same format and the same underlying values as most of the cartoons. The "good guys" or "super heroes" always win. The message is clear, the most powerful are the strongest, smartest, and fastest at drawing their guns, i.e., the most able to *inflict pain or death*.

For some of us, the ideas that the strongest wins or that might is right are troublesome. If instead we say "might for right," it sounds somewhat more palatable. This is the shift attempted by King Arthur in the legendary story of the Kingdom of Camelot. With coaching from his mentor, the magician Merlin, the newly crowned King Arthur decided that the perpetual contests among knights to establish their places in the hierarchy were not very constructive. Instead Arthur instituted a round table, which inferred no hierarchy. Furthermore he tried to channel the knights' fighting activities into efforts for good, such as defending vulnerable women. The knights, however, didn't get the point of the round table and turned even the quest for justice and fairness into a contest for domination.

I wonder whether King Arthur would fare any better in today's boardrooms with his round table and attempts to change how people view power. I wonder whether the behavior of the knights was substantially different from those modern-day heroes who make the use of violence into a virtue, or those whose good works are motivated (perhaps unconsciously) by a desire to earn a higher status in the eyes of God or the community or the corporation. If not approached carefully, even a developing sense of spirituality can be turned into a kind of spiritual elitism, a phenomenon common enough to be given the name *"spiritual materialism."*

Basically Merlin was suggesting to Arthur that the dominator model of power didn't work—that a hierarchy based on might (ability to inflict harm) was bound to fail. "Why?" you may wonder. "After all, isn't survival based on being the fittest, the strongest, and the most capable of defeating the competition?" I know that's what we've always assumed. On closer examination, however, could it not be exactly the opposite— might the very survival of the human species, indeed of the whole planet, depend on *cooperation* instead of *competition?* It was, after all, the ability of single-celled organisms to live and work together in cooperation that allowed the evolution of more and more complex multi-celled organisms. Is it not possible, then, that cooperation among the individual members of the body of humanity will be a key factor in the future evolutionary success of our species?

Power as Status

Of all the different types of power, I think the power assumed to be conferred by status is the most addictive. The various attributes of status are things we believe we need in order to achieve and maintain a suitable place within some hierarchical ranking system. The ranking may be based on wealth, possessions, prestige, physical attributes (e.g., appearance or athletic prowess), education, ethnicity, title, or some combination of such factors. In other words, status is relative. You can never have too much status, and you can always aspire to having more, so that you can move up in the hierarchy or protect your position against a competitor.

Climbing the Ladder

Judging and labeling people (including oneself) so that each can be assigned a place in some ranking system turns out to occupy a lot more of our mental energy than most of us realize. When I paid close attention to my own thoughts for a period of time, I was dismayed to discover that my mind seemed to be almost totally preoccupied with judgmental thoughts. "To what purpose?" I wondered. Then I realized that it was all so that I could fit myself onto the power spectrum and feel good about the fact that there were others lower on the scale than I was. Of course there are also always people higher on the scale, so in the end I only reconfirmed my underlying belief in my relative powerlessness! At the same time I convinced myself that all I needed to feel better about myself was more of the attributes that confer status and move one up the power ladder.

I have also had the opportunity to observe how uncomfortable people feel when placed in an environment where everyone appears equal—where there is no apparent power structure. The medical school in which I taught had neither formal lectures nor examinations. Although the students enjoyed the freedom to learn in their own way and their own time, many had a hard time adjusting to the absence of any grading or ranking system. I suppose this is a natural response of anyone (not just students) for whom their place on the ladder is a major contributor to their sense of identity. After all it's hard to feel good about yourself based on the amount of status you have, if you have no way of assessing or defining your status.

Presumably that's why we're all so interested in who has what status. We want to get for ourselves more of that sweet feeling of success, that powerful feeling you have when you think you're in control, and that proud feeling of winning. So desperately do some people crave these warm feelings that they end up sacrificing nearly all their time and energy to satisfy this craving. This addiction shows up in myriad disguises. Some, like the hard-driving (workaholic) business executive, the feisty politician, and the perfectionist housekeeper, are regarded by society as respectable. Others, like the gambler, abuser, or gangster, are not respected. The motivations and accompanying assumptions, however, are the same; "If I can just acquire the attributes of status, then I will have the power to control circumstances to my advantage; others will look up to me (perhaps even be afraid of me), and I will feel happy and affirmed."

This is the same belief summed up by Tevye in the musical *Fiddler on the Roof* (lyrics by Sheldon Harnick) when he sings, "if I were a rich man. . . ." It's not just that he wants more time "to sit in the synagogue and pray." He wants other people "to come and fawn on [him]" because, as he puts it, "when you're rich they think you really know." Even though our rational minds can acknowledge that status alone cannot confer real and lasting power, this belief still persists deep in our subconscious minds. Like the addict whose experience shows that the "high" is not only temporary but also illusory, we maintain the behavior because, in another part of our brains, all of us believe that there is no other way to achieve what we so desperately want.

Seeking Power through Possessions

Seeking to obtain power and its assumed benefits through the acquisition and accumulation of *possessions* is a very common manifestation of the assumption that material status is an accurate measure of power. Losing our possessions, then, is tantamount to losing our power, perhaps even our identity. No wonder we become so desperately *attached* to our possessions!

This possessiveness extends into every part of our lives. It accounts for the exclusiveness that undermines our attempts at teamwork and the quality of our relationships with our children, spouse, friends, and employees. Most of the people with whom I have spoken about this immediately deny that they feel any ownership of children, spouse, friends, or employees. While I accept that they are speaking the truth as far as their conscious mind is concerned, the language that all of us use consistently betrays our subconscious beliefs. The words may be subtle, but they are words of ownership nonetheless. Here are a few examples—see if you can add some of your own. In the marriage ceremony (granted less frequently now than in the past) the bride is "given away," and we "take [our partner] to *have* and to hold." Love songs frequently refer to the beloved as "mine, all mine," and jealously threaten anyone who might "steal" their beloved from them. One example is the song *Every Breath You Take* (The Police, A&M Records, 1996), which asserts "you belong to me." In the same way, corporations feel a sense of ownership over their employees, perhaps because they feel they have purchased them; likewise, some employees feel as if they had "*sold their soul*" to the company.

Ownership implies control or power over. Therefore, it is perhaps not surprising that disappointment, anger, and even violence frequently erupt when the boss, parent, or lover discover that they can't control the person whom they assumed they had a right to control by virtue of ownership (although they probably wouldn't express it that way). In the case of children, that might be the point at which parents *disown* their child. It might equally be the assumption behind many cases of abuse, whether of children, spouse, or employees.

✴ *An Opportunity for Personal Reflection* ✴

Make a list of your words, actions, and reactions that might reveal underlying feelings of possessiveness toward your children, significant other, or employees.

Which of your possessions give you the greatest feeling of elevated status?

How would you feel if those possessions were vandalized or if you lost them?

What is the something that, if you had it (or more of it), would help you feel more powerful?

Of course, in our conscious, rational minds we know full well that we can't own another person. The idea of ownership of persons should have died with the practice of slavery. I'm suggesting, however, that slavery is far from dead; it simply takes different forms today. For example, Marjorie Kelly in her book *The Divine Right of Capital, Dethroning the Corporate Aristocracy,* says of the idea of "employees-as-property" that "evidence of it is widespread as in the commonplace observation that 'employees are our greatest asset'."

I suggest that the reason slavery still exists is that in our subconscious minds we still think of employees, spouses, and children as possessions—part of our power base. For example, we may believe we have "bought" an employee with stock options, bonuses, or special treatment of some sort. Because we believe we own other people, we believe we are justified in controlling them, making demands on them, exploiting them, and possibly even abusing them. There is, then, at the very least, a need for these unconscious beliefs to be made explicit and reframed, so that our automatic, habitual behavior can come into line with what we say we believe.

There are also very practical reasons for changing our thinking and the resultant behavior—people who are treated as possessions are not the most effective or loyal employees. Spouses and children who are treated as possessions are not likely to react with love. Love, respect, loyalty, and cooperation cannot be purchased or owned. In *The Prophet,* Kahlil Gibran makes a similar point when he says:

> Your children are *not your* children,
> They are the sons and daughters of Life's longing for itself.
>
> They come through you but not from you,
> And though they are with you yet *they belong not to you.*

(ITALICS MINE)

Similarly we might do well to remember that employees and colleagues are not ours, nor do they belong to the corporation. They are persons with separate rights to self-determination and self-realization. It is our privilege to share part of their journey and to contribute to their growth and development even as they contribute to our growth and our goals.

Can Power Really Be Achieved through Status?

When I ask my clients to search their hearts and tell me what is ultimately of most importance to them—what they value most in life—what they would like to have written in their obituary—they usually mention relationships, shared love, a sense of fulfillment, and living out their unique purpose in life. Yet when these same people make a pie chart of how they apportion their time and energy, a very different picture usually emerges. Why is there so often this discrepancy between thought and action? It's not that their conscious mind doesn't really want those things; it's because the subconscious mind that directs their automatic behavior is operating on a different set of beliefs. In other words, unless you consciously choose otherwise, your subconscious beliefs are running your life.

A common belief is that all you need in order to achieve happiness, fulfillment, and peace of mind, is to get hold of power in the form of status—if you accumulate sufficient prestige and possessions, what you really want will follow. Some of my clients told me that they had debunked this myth the hard way. After laboring a lifetime and sacrificing much to climb the ladder of success, they still found their victories hollow. Because the status they had obtained had been powerless to deliver what they most wanted in life, they ended up feeling cheated.

✳ An Opportunity for Personal Reflection ✳

In what ways do you seek personal and professional status?
What do you value most in life?
Are your status-seeking strategies bringing you what you most value
and most desire in life?

Summary

In the prevailing paradigm, power is often defined in **quantitative** terms: How much money? How many friends? How popular? How strong? How many people report to you? How much wealth do you manage? How large an arsenal do you have? Quantitative measurement is important because it allows us to make comparisons—to place people, corporations, nations, and most importantly ourselves, on the power ladder. Power ranking gives us a method for evaluating every person and every situation. The assessment of power in the prevailing paradigm has little concern with either the effectiveness or the quality of the power being measured. For example, is the power being measured effective in making happen what you want to happen on a sustainable basis? What is the quality of the relationship if it is based on a power differential?

Although usually assumed to be measures of power, authority, control, strength, and status, when considered critically, all turn out to be more about creating the illusion of power than the real thing. As long as we cling unquestioningly to the prevailing assumptions when defining and measuring power, we will only perpetuate the illusion of power and will deny ourselves the effectiveness and joy of being *authentically powerful*.

CHAPTER 3

What Is Authentic Power?

I f *authentic* power is not primarily about authority, control, strength, or status, what is it about? How can we recognize and measure authentic power, and what makes it more effective in translating our deepest desires into reality on a sustainable basis? These questions are not easy to answer. In the first place extremely few people have ever fully succeeded in their quest to reach authentic power. Secondly those who have managed to raise their consciousness sufficiently to get occasional glimpses of authentic power have had a hard time communicating their wisdom to us, so fixated are we on pursuing power as defined by the conventional view.

There are many similarities between the concept of authentic power and what Abraham Maslow called "self-actualization" (See, for example, *Self-Actualizing People: a Study of Psychological Health*). Not surprisingly, therefore, Maslow had the same difficulty in finding self-actualized people to study and describe as I am to describe fully developed, authentic power. His strategy to get around this problem was to study people in the *process of self-actualizing*. Even then, he found that only one in three thousand college students met his criteria (i.e., who were far enough along in the process to be considered "self-actualizing").

In this chapter I offer some *clues* by which you may recognize authentic power when you catch glimpses of it. I have derived this description of authentic power from a combination of sources, such as the lives of certain "exemplary" historical figures or "masters", the work of people like Abraham Maslow, and the wisdom distilled from my own observations. I encourage you to make your own observations of people who appear to be further along in their quest for authentic power than you are—who are closer to being able to achieve what is most important to them in a sustainable fashion—to draw your own conclusions, and to modify accordingly the composite picture presented here.

Power as Authenticity

Whereas the conventional view assumes that power is associated with the *role* you play or the *position* you hold, the paradigm of authentic power recognizes that real power is evidenced when you are *real*—when you are true to your *authentic Self*. I will use an upper case "S" when referring to the authentic Self and its synonyms, *true Self, higher Self, transpersonal Self, Source, Soul*, etc. in order to distinguish it from the concept of self generated by all our subconscious beliefs and assumptions. Sometimes referred to as our "ego", this collection of beliefs and assumptions came originally from other people and our own limited interpretation of our experiences. Because the notion of self generated by these beliefs is not representative of who we really are, it could more accurately be called our "pseudo self."

Authenticity might, at first, seem like a strange way to characterize power, especially in a world so caught up in the illusion created by our insecure and fearful egos. The self that the ego projects is its own creation; it's not who we really are. Consequently the more we allow our egos to define who we are, the more disconnected we become from the reality of our power. Most of us have come to identify so strongly with the various masks and personae created for us by our egos, that we have completely lost touch with our real Selves.

Authentic power is evidenced only as we reconnect with our true Selves and allow that part of us to direct our lives. In other words, *authentic power comes from being authentic*. The authentic Self is the only *authority* we need to be truly powerful; it is the Source of true power. This means that the power of authenticity is available to everyone. It is not reserved for a special few, nor does it have to be won in a competition or struggle; it is already a part of you.

With authority, as we have seen, comes *respons-ibility*, which is not power but duty masquerading as power. With authenticity, however, comes *respons-ability*. This *ability to respond* appropriately and creatively to situations as they arise is real power. It is distinct from both the *duty* to respond and the relatively power-deficient, common practice of simply *reacting* to situations in some habitual, preprogrammed fashion, as I will elaborate on later in this book.

You might not have recognized the power of authenticity, even if you have glimpsed it, because it tends not to draw attention to itself and it is not necessarily associated with high profile positions or titles. Authenticity doesn't need that. Instead, the power of authenticity is *quietly efficient* and *confidently effective*. People who are more authentic than most, (those Maslow calls "self-actualizing") can be found if you look for them. They are not restricted to any particular level in an organization or any particular role in society. They are people living their purpose, people providing leadership but not caring who gets the credit, and people who understand that "who they are makes a difference." They are not wasting their energies climbing ladders, being fearful of future possibilities, regretful of the past, or resisting the present. They are focused on living fully and authentically NOW—each and every moment.

This way of living, in which someone is in harmony with the deepest values of his or her soul, is sometimes described in terms of *integrity*. This term is used by both Steven Covey in describing "principle-centered leaders" and by Abraham Maslow as a characteristic of "self-actualizing" people. The term *integrity* signifies that the person's words, actions, and values are all *integrated* together under the influence of that part of themselves that is beyond the ego—beyond the mind. All the things that truly matter to people—beauty, love, creativity, joy, and inner peace—come not from the mind or the ego, but from that part I call the authentic Self.

A more figurative representation of what it means to be authentic is to speak of *integrating head and heart*. To be effective (powerful) we need both. The mind, as represented by the head, functions as an excellently *efficient administrator*, but a very poor *director*. When left alone the mind relies on its subconscious belief system (ego) to make choices. These are the automatic choices that we don't have to think about.

The trouble with "running on automatic" is that before you know it, your ego is virtually running your life, choosing your emotional and behavioral reactions, and judging everyone by its own standards. You are not in control of your own life—your ego is! On the other hand, *when the administrative capability of the mind (head) is used to serve the deep desires of the heart (representing the authentic Self), then efficiency is combined with effectiveness, and you experience the power of being authentic.* I refer to the heart, not as some wishy-washy, sentimental entity, but rather as representing the very essence of who you are—the authentic You. When head and heart are working in cooperation, body, mind, and soul are working as one—thought, word, and deed are in harmony. This shows itself as integrity and authenticity, and where there is authenticity, there is authentic power.

✳ *An Opportunity for Personal Reflection* ✳

What is it that makes some people appear "phony?"

Do you know people who would justify any means to get what they wanted even if that meant going against their own values?

Do you know people who would stick to their values even if it meant loss of friends, loss of job, or other hardships?

In what people (historical, fictional, and contemporary) have you glimpsed authenticity? What other words could you use to describe these people?

Power as Synergy

One important aspect of the power of synergy is that, like other forms of cooperation, it implies *power with*—with other people, with the environment, etc. This contrasts with the assumption of the prevailing paradigm that power is associated with exerting *control over* people, over situations, over the economy, over the environment, etc. The underlying motivation for control tactics is actually *fear*, whereas the power of synergy comes from *respectful, honoring relationships*.

Synergy implies something more powerful than what is achieved through simple collaboration, cooperation, or teamwork. These words all refer to working together. We are familiar with the benefits of working together, as captured in the expressions "two heads are better than one" and "many hands make light work." Generally we interpret such expressions to mean that the output is directly proportional to the input. Synergy, however, describes the situation when the *outcome is greater than the sum of the individual contributions*. It happens when each contributor is enabled to be more—more effective, more vital, more authentic, more alive—when in association with one or more others than the same person is alone. No one is drained or diminished. In other words, *synergy is a shared experience of authentic power.* Consequently, synergy results in *both* inspired individual performances *and* inspired team performances.

Often when we use terms such as *"inspired performance"* or *"peak performance,"* we are using them in the context of competitiveness. In describing synergy, however, I am concerned only with the phenomenon by which some quality of a relationship enables, encourages, and inspires *all parties* in the relationship to "be more" than they would otherwise be. Perhaps the authentic power, when it is experienced as synergy, would better be described as "peak participation in life." In contrast, when one or more party in a relationship is motivated by need or greed, the relationship will be characterized by attempts to dominate or exploit the others. Instead of all parties in the relationship being enriched and experiencing the feelings of joy and fullness of life that are characteristic of a growing self-actualization (authenticity), parties in these exploitative, dependent, or co-dependent relationships experience only an increasing sense of poverty, powerlessness, and resentment. In other words, the net output is *less* than the sum of the inputs.

The exact nature of the *inspiration* involved in producing synergy is difficult to pin down. Certainly it is not simply what we call *charisma. Rapport* might be a better word to describe the subtle connection that forms among people in a synergistic relationship and that is experienced, at least partially, at the *intuitive* level. Members of teams speak of experiencing moments of synergy as an ability to be in perfect synch with the thoughts and actions of the other members without the need for verbal or written communication—things just gel, and desired outcomes seem to happen almost effortlessly.

Synergistic relationships and the power that is associated with them are not limited to any particular sphere of life.

Synergy in your own life happens when every part of your life is perfectly in step with every other part. It allows you to optimally combine your knowledge, wisdom, and skills to create the kind of life that you most value and desire. Synergy can also result from the relationship among persons, groups, and nations, and between each of these and the environment. It doesn't matter that one party is a corporation or has a title like manager, coach, husband, or mother, while the other party is the environment, an employee, a player, a wife, or a child. The rankings and the power ladder to which we are so accustomed in the status-based prevailing paradigm simply have no place in the paradigm of authentic power.

✳ *An Opportunity for Personal Reflection* ✳

Have you ever experienced or witnessed this kind of "inspired performance?" If so, how do you account for this phenomenon?
Do you know any married couples or close friends who operate together in this way?

Power as Inner Strength

Authentically powerful people appear to draw on some invisible, ill-defined strength that could be called inner strength or resourcefulness. In several respects, this inner strength can be differentiated from the kind of strength associated with the conventional view of power. What I am characterizing as inner strength comes from a sense of wholeness, self-worth, and therefore, trust in one's self. Inner strength often seems to radiate from those who possess it—sometimes revealing an inner beauty—sometimes spreading a sense of calm—always illuminating those present. In contrast, the strength that the prevailing paradigm associates with power is a by-product of the ego's sense of incompleteness, neediness, and fear. The resulting competing, grasping, threatening, fighting, and bullying may produce the illusion of power, but in reality these are expressions of *weakness*.

People naturally respond to such a show of strength with resistance of some type (defensiveness or counterattack, for example). Inner strength, on the other hand, is not threatening. People tend to respond to inner strength by wanting to associate more closely with those who exhibit it. By the same token people who have what I am calling *inner strength* do not themselves easily feel afraid or threatened. Because their strength comes from inside themselves, they are secure in the knowledge that *no outside force, act, opinion, or label can diminish them.* They do not depend on the affirmation or validation of others. Uninhibited by the insecurities that motivate others, such people are free to be themselves. This is the aspect of authentic power that I call *inner strength.*

In addition to the confident resourcefulness and quiet effectiveness that are part of inner strength, there can also be what we tend to regard as special gifts or *powers:* intuitive powers, the power to affect outcomes without physical intervention, creative powers, and the power to draw to oneself what one truly needs. These powers, however, are not restricted to any elite group, nor are they earned, won, or bought. As with all aspects of inner strength, these powers are part of the birthright of every person. Those all-too-few individuals who have connected with *the Source* of this inner strength (i.e., their true, indestructible Essence), understand the futility of power struggles and the hollowness of victories won by show of strength; they have found a strength that is far more effective, more real, and closer at hand—they have found the authentic power of inner strength.

✳ *An Opportunity for Personal Reflection* ✳

Imagine how you would feel if you were immune to all fears and anxieties.

Imagine no longer needing acceptance or affirmation from others.

What else might change in your life if you were able to be confident, unafraid, and independent of the opinion of others?

Power as Quality of Being

What on earth is "quality of being", and how can that be an aspect of authentic power? Admittedly, for the vast majority of us who are accustomed to precise, quantifiable terms, the words "quality of being" seem hopelessly vague, perhaps even meaningless. Certainly they are not very helpful to anyone caught up in constantly striving for higher status as a means to power. That such people should find this an alien concept is not surprising, because quality of being is something that the mind (ego) cannot grasp, much less produce. As with the other aspects of authentic power, quality of being cannot be attained through intellectual activity. Quality of being refers to the *experience* of joy, ease, and serenity that derive from identification with one's authentic Self or *inner Being*. Surely this is the state of being that we all long to achieve, and as such, is this not worthy of the designation *authentic power?*

The conventional view, by contrast, assumes that power is associated with *status*, which it measures by the extent of *doing* and *having*—so much so that our species might better be described as *human doings* or *human havings*. People who measure themselves and others by how much they have and how much they do commonly get so caught up in competing for status based on these criteria that they succumb to burnout, heart attacks, and other stress-related disorders. How powerful is that?

Does this mean that people who enjoy this quality of being don't *have* or *do* anything? Of course it doesn't mean that. What distinguishes a person whose focus is on expressing his *inner Being* is that he is free from control by his ego. He is not acting out of fear; neither is he striving for status or other forms of recognition. Therefore his attention is 100% focused on what's happening in the *present moment*, without such distractions as judgmental thoughts, ownership issues, concern for what the outcome will be, or resistance to what's happening. The assumptions of the prevailing paradigm would lead us to believe that a person whose primary focus is on *being in the moment* would be ineffectual. The truth, surprisingly, is that this *way of being* is associated with a very high degree of both efficiency and effectiveness. Indeed this is why I have characterized it as an aspect of *authentic power*.

✳ An Opportunity for Personal Reflection ✳

By what criteria do you measure yourself and your life?

To what extent is your identity tied up in your career, your home, your reputation, and your possessions?

Have you ever gotten away from the stress of trying to impress others and to meet their expectations? Can you recall even brief moments of serenity and joy? Imagine your whole life being like those special moments.

Summary

Authentic power is not amenable to being measured in quantitative terms as we are accustomed to doing. Instead it is recognized by such things as the *quality* of the relationships where it is at play and the joyful, stress-free quality of life that attends it. It is described in terms of authenticity, synergistic relationships, inner strength, and overall quality of being. External attributes, possessions, and actions are transitory, and the power they represent is illusory. By contrast, *inner power* is both lasting and real because it is identified with the authentic, non-destructible Self. As such it is effective in providing what we truly desire— and doing so on a sustainable basis, which is after all, the only true measure of power.

CHAPTER 4

The Conventional View of How Power Is Obtained

G iven the significance in our lives of power and our result-ing preoccupation with the quest for power, what could be more strategically important than knowing where and how to find what we are looking for and then how to acquire it? We all base our quest, whether we realize it or not, on key assump-tions about the source and nature of power. When these com-mon assumptions about power have been made explicit, you may recognize their inadequacies and realize that they are actu-ally limiting you in your quest for authentic power.

Power as a Commodity

One of the reasons that, as a society, we are so preoccupied with the quest for power is that we assume that power is a *scarce commodity*. We treat power like we treat money—as if there were a finite amount of power in the world and as if power were unevenly distributed among individuals, corporations, and countries. Obtaining power, then, becomes a matter of redistribution and the creation of a better (more stable) balance of power. None of this struggle to redistribute power would be necessary, of course, if power were not actually a commodity. If we assume (as most of us do) that power is something *external* to us, something that can be *transferred* from one person to another, as well as something that is in short supply, then it is only natural that we look to whomever or whatever controls the power when we look to increase our share of it.

Presumably the power that is assumed to come with position or status is controlled by someone higher up in the hierarchy—someone with more power. Likewise wealth is controlled by someone who has more of it than you do; knowledge is controlled by experts; and so on. If you look back at the list you rated in terms of power in Chapter 1, you will likely note that, to whatever extent these people were perceived to have power, the source of that power was something *external*. Even strength, good looks, and athletic ability are all external in the sense that they can be lost. Even then the *essential person* would still exist. Isn't that what we mean by the expression "beauty is only skin deep?" Nevertheless, it is natural in our society to attribute power to people who possess these external or superficial attributes.

Seldom do we stop to think that the apparent power of individuals with these special attributes could simply be the result of our *assuming* they had that power, and then treating them as if they did! If, for example, we look to medical professionals for the source of healing or to religious leaders and gurus for the source of spirituality, then it may be we who are creating that image of power—it is not necessarily intrinsic by virtue of their expertise. When we think of divine power, whether we name that power as "God" or any other name, we are accustomed to thinking of that power as "up there" or "out there" somewhere. We similarly *bestow on others the power* to tell us who we are, to define what is right and wrong for us, and to determine our emotional status by granting or withholding validation and affirmation.

So accustomed are we to looking outside ourselves for the source of power that it would not even occur to us to consider the possibility of a different kind of power—one that originates *inside* us. Might this limitation account for the fact that, in spite of a lifelong quest, most people have not discovered *authentic power*—only occasional facsimiles?

There is a fable about creation that suggests this is indeed why authentic power keeps eluding us. It seems that the gods were meeting to settle the final details of creation before the big event. The question to be resolved was, "Where shall we hide the secret of life so that humans will not be able to find it?"

"Perhaps we should bury it beneath the tallest mountain," suggested one of the gods. At first this seemed like a good solution to their dilemma, however, the more they thought about it, the more they realized its shortcomings. They had designed humans to be pretty inventive, so sooner or later humans would figure out how to tunnel under even the tallest mountain. The secret of life would certainly not be safe there!

The same kind of reasoning caused them to reject the second idea, which was to place the secret at the bottom of the deepest ocean. It seemed to them that no place would be safe from discovery by humans. Finally they managed to hit on what they all agreed was a foolproof plan. They decided to hide the secret to life inside the humans, knowing that no one would ever think to look there for it.

The assumption that power can be transferred from one individual to another, when coupled with the ideas that power is a scarce commodity and that it originates outside us, is behind both the notion of a power struggle or competition and the idea that one individual can empower another. The power described by these assumptions, however, may be more illusion than reality.

✻ An Opportunity for Personal Reflection ✻

When is the last time someone gave you power? I don't mean "authority." I don't mean someone saying that they were "empowering" you. I mean the ability to translate intention into reality on a sustainable basis.

Have you ever witnessed this kind of power being seized from someone else?

We can all think of examples where the balance of power seemed to shift. What really happened though? Did power change hands like some commodity? More likely what was seized was not power but the ability to make more convincing or more serious threats than the person who appeared to lose power. An example would be an arms race in which the country with the greatest fire-power is said to be the most powerful. Actually they are not the most powerful, simply the most feared. The same could be said of the tough boss. In any case, no commodity called *power* is transferred to the strong nation from the weak one or to the tough boss from the fearful employee.

If, as I am suggesting, the assumption that power is transferable is actually false, then neither empowerment nor power struggles would make any sense. Furthermore, if there were plenty of power for everyone because it already resided in ample quantity inside each of us, there would be little need to transfer it anyway!

Power as a Reward

Most people work and play, in fact live their whole lives, as if life were a game or competition to be *won*. Winning is equivalent to succeeding, and it is assumed that power is the first reward of the winners. What do those we brand as "losers" get—a consolation prize of some sort? No, the losers get only our contempt and scorn—that is just how the game goes.

✳ *An Opportunity for Personal Reflection* ✳

To what do you look forward when you strive to succeed?
Against whom are you competing?
Who will "lose" if you win? If you succeed?

Perhaps this is why the concept of *win-win* is so hard to grasp. How can everyone *win* if winning is understood to mean " making the other party lose?" According to that way of think-ing, surely *win-win* would be the same thing as *lose-lose*. It is not surprising then, that while some may pay lip service to the notion of *win-win*, generally we take our *win-lose* attitude into everything from our domestic disagreements to international affairs.

Whether we win an argument, a game, a contract, or a war, there are always losers. It may sound like a laudable goal to make your business or your nation more competitive, but what you are really doing at the same time is making other compa-nies or nations into losers. According to this assumption, then, the process of winning and losing whether the contest is an obvious power struggle or not—is really the process of transfer-ring power from one party to another. In winning we are attempting to gain power at someone else's expense. It's won-derful to be a winner, but nobody wants to be a loser!

At best, the assumption that power can be won makes life into a game or competition. At worst, it keeps us in a constant struggle or battle for survival. "That's okay," we conclude, "because that's how the universe works—survival of the fittest. The winners (whether individual, corporate, or national) deserve to succeed, whereas the losers should be weeded out." According to Charles Darwin, it was winning at this game that got us to the top of the evolutionary ladder. It's an easy step to extend the concept from evolution to winning in sports battles, in economic battles, in domestic disputes, and in warfare between nations. If that's how evolution works, that's how business should work. And that's how all of society should work—the winners shall inherit the earth!

There are, however, other possibilities I'd like you to consider. What if we are so much into the game that we fail to consider that the whole notion of winning at someone else's expense is a kind of illusion? What if we've gone as far as we can with survival of the strongest and that to go further would put the human species in danger of being wiped out altogether? What if the survival of humans was tied instead to the raising of our consciousness? What if, like the chicken and the egg, our assumptions about power and winning keep us from achieving a higher level of consciousness, while not being able to view things from that higher plane keeps us from seeing that the notion of winning is only an illusion? What if being the strongest wasn't the same as being the fittest as we have been assuming?

Before you completely dismiss these questions, consider this story. It's a story that I saw on a 16 mm film many years ago. It caused me to reconsider my own beliefs. The story is about two hand-puppets named Stripes and Spots. The two are the best of buddies; they live next door to each other and enjoy playing and doing just about everything together. After all, as Stripes observed, "We have so much in common; we even look alike."

"That's right," replied Spots, gazing fondly at his friend, "we both have stripes. . . ."

"I think you mean that we both have spots," interrupted his counterpart.

After escalating the argument for a while, they attempted to prove their respective points by looking in a mirror. What they discovered in the process were their differences. One indeed had stripes and the other spots! Immediately mistrust, and later fear, came between these long-time friends, to the extent that they felt the need to erect a fence between their properties. Gradually they became more and more suspicious of each other and began to fortify in case the other might be planning an attack.

Eventually armed combat broke out between them, at which point each, fearing defeat at the hands of his old friend, sought allies in the conflict. Inevitably each puppet started looking up the arm that was close by. Discovering the face of the puppeteer, each in turn, tried to make a case why the puppeteer should fight on his side. "If you love me," each pleaded, "protect me from my enemy." How could the puppeteer make them understand that he loved them equally and that a defeat for either of them would be a defeat for all three—both puppets and the puppeteer? Finally he suggested to each that they continue to look past his face and down the opposite arm. Of course in this way each discovered that, in spite of differences, each was part of the same larger whole.

At a certain level of consciousness, perhaps we would also discover that, although each of us is unique, we are all parts of the same body—the body of humanity! From this perspective, winning and losing make no more sense than for my right arm to win in a fight with my left arm. It would be as ridiculous as your brain cells and liver cells, given their very different appearances and not aware that they possessed identical DNA, fighting to the death. In order for your body to be healthy, all the cells in your body must work together in harmony. If this fails to happen, as in the case of cancer where certain cells take what might be compared to a win-lose attitude, disease of the whole body is the consequence.

From this perspective there is no such thing as win-lose. That being the case, is there really any sense in talking about winning or losing at all, and is perhaps the disease affecting the body of humanity simply that its various parts are competing with each other? If, at some level, all people are part of the same whole, then the notion of wresting power away from someone else will need to be rethought. So, too, will the idea of empowering another person by voluntarily giving up some of our power.

Summary

According to the conventional view, power is a commodity. It is in scarce supply and unevenly distributed among people; however, like other commodities, power can be bought, sold, given, won, or seized. This view of power assumes power to be external to the individual and transferable from one person to another. The most common way of trying to obtain power in this paradigm is by succeeding in a power struggle, i.e., by winning it. It turns out on closer examination, however, that the notion of winning in particular and the transfer of power in general may be simply an illusion. Consequently, as we attempt to fill the places within us that seem empty of power, we find that we only increase our experiences of powerlessness.

CHAPTER 5

The Keys to Gaining Authentic Power

S uppose you are at least temporarily able to suspend whatever assumptions you may have had about how power is obtained. Suppose you accept for the moment that real power cannot be won, earned, or given, and that you already have an adequate supply within you. How do you go about gaining access to that inner power?

The answer is that certain kinds of thoughts are the key to having real power. Every thought we have is *potentially* very powerful; every thought is *potentially* creative. The growing reliance on sport psychologists is testimony to the power of the mind, in this case to influence athletic performance. You don't have to be a professional athlete, however, to have seen the power of the mind demonstrated. Anyone who has ever stood at the golf tee and thought about the likelihood of their ball landing in the water hazard has probably experienced the power of their thoughts to affect outcomes. This power of thought is not limited, though, to golf or even sports; it operates in every sphere of human experience and endeavor. The power of thought is not limited to any elite group. It is not a scarce commodity to be competed for. Because it is intrinsic to everyone, the power of thoughts can be used to facilitate any kind of desired outcome, by any person, regardless of status, strength, or intellect.

The Power of a Strong, Clear *Intention*

Intentions are an especially powerful kind of thought. This claim may surprise you, particularly if you have noticed that there is often a disconnect between people's stated intentions and what they actually end up doing. Because of this, intentions have developed a bad name; it is said, for example, that "the road to hell is paved with good intentions." The ineffectiveness of intentions, however, is not because intentions lack power. On the contrary, a strong, clear intention is the best way I know to access your power. First let me describe the distinguishing features of a truly powerful intention, and then I will explain why our intentions so often appear impotent.

The Nature of Intentions

Each intention is associated with a *desired goal or outcome*. Usually these thoughts take the form of a mental image of that outcome having been already achieved. For example, several years ago I had an intention to publish a book. I imagined what it would be like to be a published author, to be present at the launch of the book, and what I would like the reaction of the readers to be.

Beyond having an identifiable outcome, intentions can be distinguished from each other by two other characteristics that I find it helpful to represent diagrammatically with arrows called *vectors*.

- The *motivation or purpose* behind the intention is represented by the direction the vector points.
- The *strength* of an intention is represented by the length of the vector.

It is important to be very clear on your motivation if your intention is to be as powerful as you would like it to be. You clarify your motivation by asking yourself, "*Why* exactly do I want to achieve this particular goal?" The direction that the arrow points in the diagram is a way to indicate the particular *motivation* or *purpose* behind the intention. A single intention, such as my intention to have a book published, could have several different motives. My purpose might have been to gain public acclaim. It might have been to share valuable insights with as many others as possible. Each motive would have its own arrow and, if several motives were involved, the diagram would include several arrows pointing in different directions even though the goal was the same for each.

The second distinguishing feature among intentions is the amount of energy or degree of *intentionality* associated with each. I call this the *strength* of the intention; it is indicated on the vector diagram by the length of the arrow used to represent it. Often we can get a clue as to the *strength* of our stated intention by paying attention to the words that we use in describing it. For example which of the following statements of intent would you represent by the longest arrow?

- "I'm going to finish this project by the end of the month, no matter what."
- "I sure would like to have this project finished by the end of the month."
- "I'll try and see if I can finish this project by the end of the month."
- "I hope this project will be finished by the end of the month."
- "It would be nice if this project were finished by the end of the month."

If I were betting on which of these people would have the project actually finished by the end of the month, there is no doubt where I would put my money. I would represent the first statement by the longest arrow. It has the most determination behind it. A statement such as the last one would have a very small arrow by comparison; it hardly has any power (*intentionality*) behind it at all. Words such as *hope* and *try* indicate that it would be okay with you if the project didn't get finished by the month's end, and since you have already given yourself permission to miss the target, chances are you will. On the other hand, a strong, clear intention can often make achievement of a goal seem almost effortless; such is the mysterious power of an intention.

The power of an intention has long been recognized in the practices of several cultures. For example the ancient Chinese healing practice called *Qigong* is based on *yi*, intent. Every Native American language has words for *healing intent*. Martial arts are also based on the correct use of *yi*. The basis of *healing prayer* is intent; the same is true for the practice of *Therapeutic Touch*, which is gaining acceptance in North America.

Exactly how intentions have their remarkable effects, even at great distances, remains largely a mystery, although there is a growing body of evidence to support the claims made for intentions. Larry Dossey, M.D., for example, has been interested in scientific demonstrations of the efficacy of healing prayer, which is one particular form of intention. What he discovered is that there were more than 130 scientific studies in the general area of "healing," many of which employ prayer. In his 1993 book *Healing Words: The Power of Prayer and the Practice of Medicine* he concluded, "not to employ prayer with my patients was the equivalent of withholding a potent drug or surgical procedure." Experiments on the effect of intent have been performed in several countries using a variety of protocols. In addition to testing the effects on humans who are subject to the power of suggestion, intent has been shown to have a statistically significant effect on plants, yeast, bacteria, and even machines.

Strong, clear intentions have such enormous power to bring about desired outcomes that a warning is in order. *Choose your intentions very carefully; otherwise, you risk producing an outcome that is not what you **really** wanted.*

My lesson in this regard was a painful one, but one that is still fresh in my mind after thirty-five years. I had been dating a girl who lived in one of the university dormitories. One evening we had planned to go to the Maple Leafs hockey game, which was within easy walking distance of where she lived. In any case, my parents needed the family car that evening. "Where's the Cadillac?" my friend asked as soon as she arrived at the front door. "Don't imagine that I want to go out with you if you don't have the Cadillac," was her response to my explanation. "Just look up at those windows," she said. "I told all those girls that I was going out with a guy who drives a Cadillac. No Cadillac—no date!"

Although my primary intention had been for her to like *me*, I cannot deny that I also intended to impress her with the car. Obviously the second intention succeeded even though I felt shattered when it did!

Why Intentions Sometimes Appear Impotent

In spite of their potential power, often even strongly held intentions fail to produce the desired outcome. They may even produce a result opposite to the one intended. Have you experienced this kind of disappointing result in spite of your good intentions? It might have been the failure to lose weight, give up an unhealthy habit, or to speak from the heart. Can you perhaps identify with the woman in the following story? It comes from any place, any day, today.

Each day of the week a woman stands at her living room window and watches the school bus stop at the end of the street. Its doors swing open, and her two children burst from the bus with coats open, scarves flying, school bags bouncing. She stands watching them, gripping the back of a wing-back chair, until her knuckles are white with the intensity of her joy. These are her children, beautiful, wondrous miracles. She feels like her heart will burst. She has no words for the feeling. When they come roaring through the doorway and she finds her words, she begins the moment the door opens. "Did you eat your lunch? Do you have any homework? You're both going to catch your death of cold running around like that! Why can't you just . . . ?" On and on she goes. What happened to the words of her heart that she wanted to tell them?

This inability to make good on our intentions and resolutions happens with sufficient frequency that we can easily conclude that, if it exists at all, the power of intention is only available to a select few—saints, gurus, or magicians. Worse still we may interpret our inability to realize our intentions as a fundamental weakness on our part. Not only is this conclusion false, it is disempowering—as feelings of guilt and failure always are.

A better explanation for the ineffectiveness of an intention is that it is being sabotaged by another, even stronger intention. The vector diagram for the intentions of the woman in the above story, for example, might look like the diagram on the next page.

If this diagram represented a tug-of-war between unevenly matched teams, you would expect that the team pulling towards the right would win i.e., the net movement would be toward the right. This is the same as saying that the net vector (the vector you get by subtracting one from the other) is a shorter one pointing towards the right. The net vector tells you which intention will be converted to outcome and how much force it will have behind it. This is why, in spite of her intention to express her love to her children, the woman ends up criticizing them.

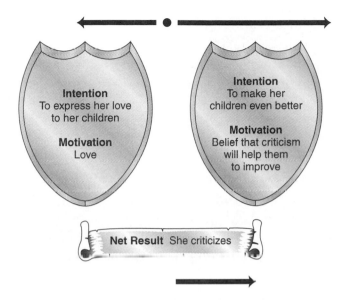

If the competing intentions had had the same strength, i.e., if they could have been represented by vectors of equal length and opposite direction, then the net vector would have been zero. Like a tug-of-war between equally matched teams where lots of energy is dissipated but no movement takes place, neither intention would bring about its goal.

It is unlikely, however, that anyone would *consciously* hold two competing intentions at the same time. Usually there is only one *stated intention* i.e., one intention of which you are consciously aware. The countervailing intention is motivated by a *subconscious* belief. Sometimes the two intentions are not completely synchronized with respect to time. In this case, just as the desired outcome is apparently within reach the other intention (which might be motivated by the subconscious belief that you don't deserve to succeed) kicks in and you move further away from your goal again. Have you ever experienced this self-sabotaging behavior in which "defeat seems to be snatched from the jaws of success?"

In real life situations, in addition to the stated intention there are usually several other intentions operating of which we are largely unaware. Consider, for example, a variety of simultaneous, interacting intentions that might be involved in how a manager relates to his or her employees.

1. **Stated intention:** to treat all employees fairly and with respect.
    Motivation: personal or corporate values.
2. **Intention:** to maintain tight control.
    Motivation: belief that employees are untrustworthy.
3. **Intention:** not to get too close to any employee.
    Motivation: belief that employees would take advantage of his friendship.
4. **Intention:** to always keep the pressure on.
    Motivation: belief that frightened employees will work harder.
5. **Intention:** to meet the bottom-line target no matter what.
    Motivation: belief that the end justifies the means.

In order to represent this combination of intentions in a vector diagram, we would also need to know the relative *strength* of each of the intentions. I have chosen to represent them in the vector diagram (shown on the next page) as only slightly different from each other in intensity.

The manner in which all these intentions interact to produce a combined outcome will depend on the strength (length) assigned to each. As I have chosen to draw them, the result is likely to be confusion or skepticism on the part of the employees. The manager's expressed values will not be consistently evident in his behavior, and it is therefore highly unlikely that the employees will feel that they are being treated fairly or with respect. The manager, who is probably unaware of the four competing intentions, will not understand why the employees

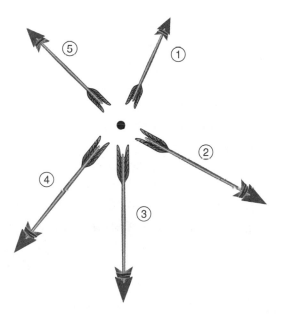

fail to appreciate what he sees only as his attempts to treat them fairly and respectfully.

Interplay among competing intentions is extremely common in all areas of our lives, and it is the main reason we don't experience the power of our stated intentions more frequently. It is also the reason why there is so often a discrepancy between our words and our deeds. In business, for example, a contradiction is frequently evident when one compares the organization's published vision and values statements with the way it actually operates. This lack of consistency arises because the stating of an intention brings it into consciousness, whereas much of our behavior consists of reacting automatically (i.e., without conscious thought) to situations as they occur. These reactions, both emotional and behavioral, are dictated by a subconscious set of beliefs, assumptions, and mental models. Eventually our actions "speak so loudly that no one hears our words!" As a result employees often become skeptical and refuse to buy in to the official statement of values. Similarly children may regard their parent's words as having little connection to reality.

The key to maximizing the power of our stated intentions lies in bringing as many of the competing intentions as possible to conscious awareness. Having done that, it is possible to consciously select the intention you really want to emphasize and to plan your strategy around it. If you think about it in terms of the diagram, this is equivalent to making one of the arrows much longer (more powerful) than all the others. Ideally you would do this process of clarifying your intentions in advance— before you go into the meeting, before you open your mouth, before you take action. It can also be used after the fact as a diagnostic tool to discover what went wrong or why your stated intention lacked power.

Consider, for example, the intentions that might be at play in simply telling someone that you love them. The obvious intention is to express your affection for that person. Suppose, however, that the person to whom you expressed these sentiments made no response of any kind. How would you feel? If you find yourself feeling cheated, then perhaps you also had an intention to receive reassurance of the other's love for you. One client told me that she always interpreted the words "I love you" to mean "I want to have sex." Possibly you intended to distract the recipient from some other love interest of which you were feeling jealous or wished to make the recipient of those words more compliant in terms of meeting your needs or expectations. Something as simple as a three-word message can be laden with all sorts of subtle or "hidden agendas." In this example, all but the stated intention were involved in trying to manipulate the recipient in some way. Once you have used this process to uncover the other intentions, you can chose to strengthen the one that matters most to you.

✳ *An Opportunity for Personal Reflection* ✳

People who are highly effective at creating what they intend are people who have learned to clarify their intention and then to maintain a high degree of focus on that intention.

Can you recall times when you amazed yourself with how much you accomplished and how things seemed to work out just the way you had hoped they would?

Did these correspond to times when you were particularly single-minded?

The Authentic Self as the Source of Real Power

The power of the mind, on its own, no matter how strong and clear the intention, is not *authentic power*. The mind, for all its surprising power, is not able to distinguish between counterfeit power and authentic power. This is because the mind is not concerned with what type of motivation we have as long as it is coupled to a strong intention. Therefore, the mind is as capable of delivering an illusion as it is of delivering authenticity; of delivering a destructive result as a constructive result, one whose goal stems from love and compassion or an outcome motivated by fear, hate, or greed. The power of the mind works as well for a killer as for a lover. This power of an intention to harm as well as to heal is amply documented by Larry Dossey in his book *Be Careful What You Pray For . . . You Just Might Get It*, which is based on his research into the power of prayer.

To be authentic, your intention needs to be aligned with your true Self. For purposes of introducing this concept, I will use the term *authentic Self* as synonymous with such terms as *true Self,* higher Self, soul, (sacred) heart, transpersonal Self—in other words the divine force (spirit) within you. Another way of thinking about authentic Self is as opposite to the false self or pseudo-self, which I have represented as a creation of the ego.

Thus, we can distinguish motivations as arising from one of two places:

- the ego, or
- the authentic Self.

In terms of the vector model, these two motivations would be represented by arrows pointing in opposite directions.

Characteristics of Intentions Motivated by the Ego

If the intention is motivated by the ego, it is represented on the vector diagram with a *downward arrow*. Its motivation is usually expressed in terms of fear, guilt, "shoulds" or "oughts," *getting* something, achieving power *over* someone, or greed. When intentions operate in the service of the ego, the results are illusory and, therefore, bring no lasting sense of satisfaction. What we all ultimately want is to feel good about ourselves, that is, to feel worthy, to be valued, to be loved. The ego operates on the assumption that this goal can only be achieved by meeting certain conditions (be perfect, work hard, be smart, be attractive, etc.), and it measures worth in terms of possessions, position, prestige, and the other trappings it associates with power. If you understand this, it becomes relatively easy to detect the intentions motivated by the belief systems that constitute the ego.

Characteristics of Intentions Motivated
by the Authentic Self

Only intentions motivated by our authentic Self are truly powerful. These intentions are represented on vector diagrams by arrows pointing *upward*. The authentic Self has nothing to prove, nothing to fear; it has no need of affirmations, no need to take credit, and no need to diminish anyone else. When the arrow representing an intention is pointing up, that means the intention is aligned with that part of us that is connected with the creative power of the universe—the universal spirit or consciousness (which we call God, *the Absolute*, the *Ground of our Being*, or a variety of other names), and which sustains, unifies, and energizes all of creation.

No wonder, then, that a strong, clear intention, which is also aligned with our unique purpose as represented by the authentic Self, is so wonderfully powerful. No wonder that it alone is capable of delivering the inner peace and sense of fulfillment that all of us seek. Furthermore this kind of power is freely available to everyone. It doesn't have to be earned or won because it comes from within. All that is necessary to realize this innate power is to put aside all the ego-generated masks, persona, and images that are keeping your authentic Self (and the power it represents) largely hidden and inoperative.

The primary motivations coming from the authentic Self tend to be oriented to the establishment and maintenance of right (respectful) relationships, not only with other people, but also with our Selves, the environment, and the Ground of our Being. This is what the soul longs for, and although we may not consciously realize it, this longing underlies all our restless striving. When we attempt to satisfy these longings by employing control and domination strategies, we end up destroying the very relationships we need in order to feel whole. Our exploitative and abusive behavior in the service of our egos results in further separation from our own true nature, from others, and from the environment. Fear, distrust, and greed, breed alienation not intimacy, hate and disdain instead of respect, and anger or frustration rather than cooperation.

Unconditional giving, because it is perfectly aligned with the authentic Self, is an extremely powerful intention. This is why there is almost no limit to what you can achieve as long as you don't mind who gets the credit for it, i.e., your motive to *give of yourself* is not contaminated with the motive of *getting* rewarded, thanked, or praised. Of course the idea of doing or giving something with no thought of payment or reward is incomprehensible to the ego.

Intentions with Mixed or Confused Motivations

Since most of the time we are under the control of the ego we seldom engage in this kind of altruistic behavior; even when we give something as simple as a smile, most of us expect a smile in return. In other words we may fool ourselves into thinking that we are giving, but in reality we are buying, trading, or investing. For example I know a couple who, every year at Christmastime give sizable gifts of money to all their children and grandchildren. This certainly has all the appearances of generous giving

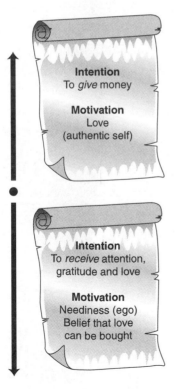

Intention
To *give* money

Motivation
Love
(authentic self)

Intention
To *receive* attention,
gratitude and love

Motivation
Neediness (ego)
Belief that love
can be bought

until I hear them two weeks later say that next year they will not give anything to those who failed to give timely thanks. The intentions involved could be represented by a vector diagram shown at the left.

Although there is clearly an arrow representing the intention *to give*, there turns out to be at least as big an arrow representing the intention *to receive* gratitude and love. In other words this couple is unconsciously trying to buy love. The net intention in this case may actually be in favor of receiving. Certainly there will be very little joy in their giving. This is, however, no isolated example. Even the motives of those children and grandchildren who express ample gratitude are probably more in the direction of ensuring that another check will be forthcoming next year. Seen in this light, very little that we think of as giving truly deserves that designation. The tragedy of this fact is that neither the giving nor the receiving is as effective as it could be.

While we all know how nice it feels to be thanked, praised, or given something, we also know how we feel when we realize that in receiving these things we have become beholden to the giver in some way. I know that, even though I appreciate being praised (it's certainly better than being criticized), I often feel that the praise is mere flattery and that it's being used to manipulate me in some way. At such times I'm much less likely to be cooperative than if I had received the praise with no strings attached. Intuitively we usually know when the praise, for example, is flattery with an ulterior motive and when it is heartfelt i.e., coming from the heart or what I have called the *authentic Self*.

As with all ego-motivated intentions, the intention *to get* is rarely as powerful (i.e., effective) as the heartfelt intention *to give*. This highlights again the paradoxical nature of authentic power *you actually receive more when your primary intention is to give than when your primary intention is to get!* Of course there is still an important place in our lives for contracts, purchases, trading, etc.; it's just that we shouldn't confuse these with the exercise of genuine power (no matter how good a bargain we are able to strike), anymore than we would confuse buying the services of a prostitute for sexual gratification, with "making love."

Another observation that can be made based on the contrast between prostitution and making love is that frequently the motivation is not obvious from the act itself. One of these acts is motivated by a desire to *get* something and therefore uses the strategy of power *over*, whereas the other is motivated, at least partly, by a desire to give or share something and uses the strategy of power *with*. In spite of their major differences, however, both are basically acts of sexual intercourse. Similarly in the example of the Christmas gifts, you can't necessarily know the motivation by looking at the check, even though the motivation (and therefore the intention) is what is ultimately of most importance.

More Important than the Action

To consider the motivation or intention behind an act as more significant than the act itself is contrary to how we are accustomed to think. What we commonly do is to take an act, which in itself is value-neutral, and attach some value to it—good or bad, right or wrong, success or failure. Worse still, we usually apply the same label to the person as we have applied to their action—the person who commits an act that we label as a crime takes on the label of "criminal." Eventually each of us ends up with labels stuck all over us, and then these labels begin to define our identity. Buried underneath all these subjective opinions and stereotypical interpretations of our *behavior* is the authentic *person*, who is neither a failure nor a success, neither a winner nor a loser, not a problem, not an agitator, and not a hero.

Labels are not a concern of the authentic Self; they are, however, a major preoccupation of the ego, which protects and defends itself against some labels while actively promoting others. Furthermore, our preoccupation with attaching judgmental labels to everything distracts us from considering more significant questions; "What are *my intentions* in this matter? Are they sponsored by the ego, the authentic Self, or some combination?" "Which of these intentions do I want to choose?" The purpose in asking these questions is not to make a judgment, but rather to increase both the efficiency and effectiveness with which we transform what we truly desire into reality by consciously choosing intentions that are aligned with the authentic Self.

In order to experience authentic power, we will need to create a unique response to each facet of each situation. The authentic Self is available to provide inspiration and intuition, but not pre-determined answers. This means, for example, carefully considering your intention/motivation for *both the action to be taken and the method by which the action is taken*.

Terminating someone's employment, for instance, may indeed be the response that is in the best interests of both the employee and the organization if the sub-standard performance is determined to be the result of a bad fit between the employee's abilities and the job requirements. Furthermore there may be no suitable match elsewhere in the organization. If some other cause for the performance gap is identified, however, it could be in the best interests of all concerned to try first to eliminate the cause of the problem. Even in those cases where termination is chosen as the response that is most consistent with the manager's authentic Self, there are still other important choices to be made, such as how, when, and where the employee will be informed. I have seen this kind of situation handled in such a way that the employee actually expresses gratitude for the decision and how it was carried out. Perhaps the employee already knows that he is in the wrong job and doesn't know what to do about it, or perhaps he just appreciates being treated with dignity and respect. In any case, this kind of outcome is surely more desirable than the alternative approach that I have witnessed being practiced in some companies. It is more satisfying for the manager because it is consistent with his authentic Self, and it is also more empowering for the employee.

Creating a unique and optimum response to each and every situation as it arises is certainly a lot more work than simply reacting automatically according to some prescribed formula, and yes, you do run the risk of being seen as inconsistent and even arbitrary by those who are fixated on rules or threatened by ambiguity. Nevertheless, taking the time and making the effort to understand other people's points of view and needs, fig-uring out what response would be in the best interest of all con-cerned, and then responding with understanding and respect for all those affected are necessary components of a successful quest for authentic power.

Summary

Perhaps the best, if not the only, way to connect to the power supply is through your thinking process. The particular thoughts that help you to access this power are called *intentions*. The clearer the intention and the freer it is from competing intentions, the more effective it will be in producing the desired outcome. Because ego-sponsored intentions tend to dominate our lives, we often squander our power on outcomes that are not what our hearts truly desire.

Authentic power is obtained by not only having strong, clear intentions, but also by ensuring that they are aligned with (sponsored by) the authentic Self. There is nothing more gen-uinely powerful than being able to live a life of purpose and meaning.

CHAPTER

What Limits
Our Power?

I f we don't consistently experience ourselves as powerful, and
if we never seem to have sufficient power (or at least as
much as we would like), it is only logical to wonder who or
what is limiting our power. The conclusions we reach in trying
to answer this question depend on our initial assumptions about
the nature and sources of power.

The Conventional Answer

Other People and Circumstances Limit Our Power

In the prevailing paradigm we have been conditioned to believe
that power is a scarce commodity; it comes as a by-product of having achieved some sort of status. Whenever we see ourselves (individually, corporately, or nationally) as less powerful than some
other party, it's only logical to conclude that we lack whatever it
takes to confer sufficient status. It could be wealth, education,
good looks, toughness, strength, connections, intelligence, and so
on, depending on our particular social milieu. Obviously it will

be different for a person in business than for a teenager and quite different again for a member of a street gang. Yet each of these groups will be trying by whatever means are at their disposal to get more of that attribute that will elevate their status and give them more power.

One consequence of having concluded that relative powerlessness is due to a personal deficiency of some kind is the tendency to become preoccupied with pointing the finger of blame, "It's my parents' fault.", "My employer is to blame." "The government did it to me.", "I didn't have the opportunities or education that others had.", "I can't help it if I have the wrong genes." The list is only limited by our imagination. Even God is not immune from being blamed!

✳ An Opportunity for Personal Reflection ✳

Who or what limits your power and holds you back from being all that you could be, from being able to experience what you most deeply desire?

In what other ways do you see yourself as a victim of fate?

Another consequence of blaming others or circumstances outside our control for our lack of power is that it promotes feelings of self-pity, jealousy, anxiety, discouragement, resentment, and resignation. It's not that there are no legitimate limitations to our power; limitations based on gender, physical disability, prejudice, etc. are all too common. It's that the process of assessing blame keeps us from moving on with our lives. The victim mentality saps resolve and strength. Eventually it becomes a self-fulfilling prophesy as people caught up in this mindset do indeed become increasingly powerless. Helping to keep people stuck in this morass are the perceived benefits of being seen as a victim. Not only does the victim get sympathy and attention, he or she is also able to exploit the sympathetic feelings of others for purposes of manipulation and control.

Sometimes we point the finger of blame at ourselves. "If only we had done something differently," we reason, "we wouldn't be in this position." We tell ourselves that "we should have known better" or "only a 'loser' would have let this happen." In this way we gradually condition ourselves to believe that we are unworthy of success.

This way of thinking is quite prevalent in our society, even among those who are regarded as successful or powerful. For many this thought process leads them to try even harder—work harder, compete harder, be more aggressive—all with the aim of compensating for their deficiencies. Some end up overcompensating for their low self-esteem; as a result they come across as aggressive, hard driving, over-bearing, arrogant, or superior.

When attempts to try harder also fail to bring about the desired outcomes, many people eventually give up trying. The combination of the bad cards they are dealt and their own stupid plays are more than they can hope to overcome. The continual berating of themselves often pushes these people from low self-esteem into apathy, depression, self-loathing, addictions, and other forms of self-abuse.

✻ *An Opportunity for Personal Reflection* ✻

Do you ever compare yourself to someone who seems to "have it all together" and think maybe it's because the other person is more deserving than you are?

What other things that you tell yourself contribute to feelings of low self-esteem and powerlessness?

In what ways do you try to remedy or compensate for these feelings?

What Actually Limits Our Experience of Authentic Power?

To say that there are *no limits* to the potential of authentic power might be overstating the matter a little, for clearly our physical bodies impose some limitations on us. Nevertheless these limitations are so miniscule in comparison to our potential powers that it would be a mistake to dwell on them at all. Certainly authentic power is so much greater than what we are accustomed to thinking of as power that the latter is not even worthy of the designation "power." Instead it is an illusion born of the beliefs and assumptions with which we have been conditioned. Since we so seldom experience this almost limitless kind of power, possibly to the point of doubting its existence, something must be limiting our power. If it's not circumstances or other people, what is it?

Our Experience of Authentic Power Is Limited by Our Own Beliefs

The limitations on our power arise largely because of the various beliefs and assumptions that we hold. We cannot experience authentic power if we are directing our quest using the assumptions of the prevailing paradigm. We will be looking in the wrong place and using the wrong techniques. For example, if we assume that power comes from some external source, we will either expect someone else to empower us or we will set about trying to win or earn more power for ourselves. Whatever power we appear to achieve by these means, however, can't get us what is really important to us because we can't force someone to love us, we can't get respect or loyalty on demand, we can't achieve true peace and security through violence, and we can't buy fulfillment.

When strategies based on these invalid beliefs about power fail (as fail they ultimately will) we assume that we have been victimized, not only by circumstances, but especially by those whom we consider to be more fortunate and, therefore, more powerful. Alternatively we may assume that we are undeserving, unworthy, or incapable of experiencing real power. In either case, the resulting victim mentality tends over time to become entrenched as another belief. This belief, like the other self-limiting beliefs, becomes a self-fulfilling prophesy. As we allow these beliefs to direct our lives, we are strengthening the very belief system that is keeping us powerless. Faced with more and more confirming evidence, the beliefs harden into facts, and we keep on going around the vicious cycle.

The potential power of an intention can be almost limitless as I elaborated in Chapter 5. Yet all that potential can be blocked or dissipated by certain common beliefs. For example, a strong intention to manage a fiscally successful operation while treating employees honestly and fairly could be disarmed by the belief that this goal is impossible to achieve. Similarly my strong intention to help people to live more fulfilling lives by writing this book could be rendered ineffective by a belief in my unworthiness to attain such a goal.

As in the case of the last two examples, our beliefs tend to raise doubts and fears in us—fear of failure, of the poor opinion of others, of loneliness, of poverty, of illness, of being hurt, and ultimately of death. Some people are even afraid of living and only stay alive because they are even more afraid of dying. The irony is that if I try to protect myself from life, I'll miss out on the rich experience of life; if I try to avoid death, I'll spend my life dying; and the more I try to exert control and domination over others, the more powerless I will end up feeling. As long as we cling to our old beliefs we will continue to live in fear, and as long as we live in fear we will continue to lack real power. Our fears and self-doubts make us susceptible to the criticisms, threats, and bribes of others so that we are easy victims of their manipulation and control tactics. Similarly it is all too easy for us as managers, parents, sales agents, etc. to exploit the fear of others as we seek to influence or control their behavior.

On the other side of the equation, consider how many great accomplishments can be attributed to people who were not intimidated by criticism, who did not equate setbacks with failure, and who refused to give up on their dream or to believe that it was impossible. Thank goodness the Wright brothers were not dissuaded from their goal by all the people who insisted that it was impossible for heavier-than-air machines to fly! This example, along with countless others, should be sufficient to convince us that you don't have to be insane like Don Quixote "to dream the impossible dream." Indeed maybe it's those of us who allow doubts, fears, and beliefs to come between us and our power who are the insane ones!

✳ An Opportunity for Personal Reflection ✳

A movie called "The Shawshank Redemption" shows the contrasting ways in which different people react to imprisonment. One character, released after many years, is unable to handle the responsibilities of freedom and greater choice. He commits suicide. The story's hero has a very different approach to life and the circumstances in which he finds himself. He refuses to allow the prison walls and barbed wire to change his attitude or defeat him. Even in prison he manages to make creative choices in circumstance where his fellow prisoners see no choice at all.

In what ways are you imprisoned by fear?

In what respects do you feel defeated, powerless, or without choice?

Can you find a way to reframe or reinterpret those circumstances— a way that opens new, creative, hopeful opportunities?

Unconsciousness Limits Our Experience of Power

The beliefs that limit our power are part of our subconscious and, therefore, we are largely *unconscious* of them. To whatever extent these beliefs are directing how we feel and how we act, we could be said to be living life unconsciously or in a kind of dream world. Since we are unconscious, we don't even realize that we have any alternatives. It might even be argued that this lack of awareness of our options is tantamount to not really having any options and, therefore, no choice. This means that *our subconscious beliefs are not only self-limiting, they are also self-perpetuating.*

The highly controlled and manipulated society depicted in George Orwell's book *Nineteen Eighty-Four* is made possible, one of the characters concludes, by a strong emphasis on "orthodoxy" i.e., staying within the prevailing paradigm. From the limited vantage point of the prevailing paradigm, people don't realize that there are any alternatives. In Orwell's story, however, Winston Smith has managed to raise his consciousness sufficiently that he understands what is happening. "Orthodoxy means not thinking—not needing to think. Orthodoxy means unconsciousness," he concludes. Referring to one of the "comrades" trapped in orthodoxy, he says "The stuff coming out of his mouth consisted of words, but it was not speech in the true sense; it was noise uttered in unconsciousness."

We are all standing on the edge of possibility, whether we realize it or not. The choice between stumbling block and stepping stone is a choice we make, perhaps hundreds of times a day. Most often these choices are made automatically, that is, unconsciously. We usually end up accepting stumbling blocks because this is the default choice—the only one offered by the prevailing paradigm. From the perspective of this paradigm, these blocks may appear like building blocks, but they are not. This is why I so often refer to the conventional view of power as illusory.

The only way out of this stalemate is to bring these limiting beliefs into conscious awareness, which simultaneously allows for the consideration of alternative, more self-empowering beliefs. This is my main purpose in writing this book—to help you raise your level of consciousness, to free you from the limitations imposed by orthodoxy, and to open up to you powerful new possibilities.

Getting past your limiting beliefs means learning to *trust* your authentic Self to help you make the choices with which you are faced. The first step in overcoming the limitations to your power is realizing that the beliefs from which you presently operate—no matter how legitimately you came by them or how widespread in society they may be—are invalid. *You do, however, have a choice.* Other, more empowering beliefs can be chosen instead. Getting past manipulation and control is first and foremost a matter of realizing that alternatives do exist. The second step is making those choices consciously, reducing as much as possible the influence of the default choices. This will produce stronger, more unidirectional intentions, and if these intentions are aligned with the authentic Self, they will be truly powerful and almost limitless. Of course if you do not *trust* the power of an intention to manifest itself—if you begin to doubt it—you will once again render the intention powerless because you have allowed a competing or limiting belief to re-assert itself.

As if it weren't already hard enough to raise our own level of consciousness, the process is further impeded by the *unconsciousness that surrounds us*. It takes courage and persistence to take the "road less traveled"—to choose intentions motivated by one's authentic Self in the face of the ego-driven behavior of the people with whom one associates day after day. The institutions in which we participate and which govern the society in which we live are generally organized around the beliefs of the old paradigm. Anyone operating from a different belief system or a different level of consciousness will make those who cannot understand feel uncomfortable, even threatened. Consequently the person attempting to break free from self-limiting beliefs risks being marginalized or punished in some way. This treatment does not have to constitute an insurmountable barrier to the achievement of authentic power. It is, in fact, typical of the reaction of those entrenched in any prevailing paradigm to an attempted paradigm shift.

In spite of the tactics of those who feel threatened by change or who are not ready to accept the responsibility of making conscious choices, this paradigm shift is underway. As I began the process of shifting my own level of consciousness—gradually questioning old beliefs and finding new insights—I was encouraged by how many people I met who were on a similar path. As I began to let go of beliefs that had kept me fearful, I became less concerned about the risks associated with not conforming to the norm (orthodoxy). I came to realize that it is people outside the norm that bring about paradigm shifts—that my own change of consciousness would ultimately help to lift everyone else. I slowly began to experience myself as more authentic and more powerful. I realized that the barriers to authentic power are products of our mindset and can, therefore, be overcome by changing our mind.

✳ *An Opportunity for Personal Reflection* ✳

Imagine the power of someone who is no longer ruled by fear, someone who is, therefore, immune to manipulation and control by others, someone who has moved to a new level of consciousness.

Imagine the quiet confidence and power of someone no longer addicted to the approval and affirmations of others, someone who is in touch with his or her authentic Self. Can you think of any current or historical examples?

Imagine having this limitless power yourself. Imagine what you could do with it.

Summary

The main barrier standing between us and the experience of authentic power is a system of beliefs that governs our personal, corporate, and political lives—beliefs of which we are largely unconscious. These beliefs breed the doubts and fears that imprison us and sabotage the power of our intentions. Since we don't know any better (i.e., we are relatively unconscious), we are easily deluded into believing that the path to authentic power lies outside ourselves in the form of status, strength, authority, or control.

Unless we accept the risks associated with breaking free to higher levels of consciousness, we will remain the prisoners of our own thinking—thinking based on the prevailing belief system. The rewards for making the mental shift to a new paradigm of power are a more fulfilling life that is increasingly based on our authentic Self and a genuine ability to confidently achieve our deepest desires.

CHAPTER 7

What Is the Conventional Way to Exercise Power?

The strategies and tactics used in the exercise of power depend on the paradigm within which you are operating. The assumptions of the prevailing paradigm result in strategies for the exercise of power that are based on control, force, and status or some combination of these approaches.

Strategies Based on Control

The most common strategies for maintaining power over people and things are based on control. The motivating emotion is usually fear. The fear takes many forms, from the fear of what others will say and the fear of failure to the fear of death. When the predominant strategy is based on being in control, however, anything that is unknown or uncertain is feared. Ultimately perhaps all these fears are related to the fear of losing control.

There are many tactics available for trying to maintain control, each with its own variations. Take intimidation, for example.

Intimidation can be as overt as bullying, but it can also be as subtle as playing to the other person's area of weakness or similar "put downs." This tactic is often employed by insecure managers to make themselves feel superior, for example, by asking a question that the manager knows the employee can't answer satisfactorily. Threats and intimidation, no matter how subtle, are still a form of abuse.

Another common tactic for maintaining control is the manipulation of information, such as the withholding of important information, the use of jargon, rumors, and propaganda. Managers for whom control is a predominant strategy will characteristically have difficulty delegating. This was certainly the case for the manager I mentioned in the Preface. Not only did he open and read employees' mail, he also threatened to fire anyone who communicated in any way with head office personnel. This meant that all dealings with our head office had to go through him personally. In this way he controlled not only the flow of information but also its content and interpretation.

Perhaps the most common method of maintaining control is the "reward and punishment" strategy—also called the "carrot and stick method." It works by the kind of psychological conditioning used to domesticate (i.e., control) animals. It is a tremendously useful technique for turning both humans and other animals into robot-like creatures whose minds have been programmed (conditioned) to react the way that someone else wants them to. It is the control technique of choice for parents, for employers, for some religions, and for society generally. Robots may be easy to control but, in turning humans into robots, the power and creativity of the human mind has been sacrificed. As a strategy for exercising *power*, therefore, it is hard to justify.

The use of carrots (incentives or rewards) and sticks (punishment or penalty) has other problems as well. Carrots motivate by appealing to greed. This means that the greediest people will be the most successful. While this approach may motivate increased effort, it also increases the likelihood of cheating, stealing, unethical behavior, lack of teamwork, and absence of loyalty. Sometimes it results in having to pay a reward just to achieve the level of performance for which the person is already being paid a salary. As demands escalate for bigger and bigger carrots this strategy could even put the organization (or family) in financial jeopardy.

Similarly, because it motivates by fear, the stick approach is likely to discourage the risk-taking necessary for creativity and instead be demotivating as well as promoting the activity known as "CYA," which is short for the colloquial expression "covering your ass." Surely approaches with so many undesirable side-effects cannot be regarded as truly effective ways to exercise power!

The use of control strategies has become so widespread and the tactics so subtle that it is difficult to objectively evaluate their effectiveness in conferring real power. Each of us is trying to exercise control over something or someone. At the same time, we are ourselves under someone else's control by virtue of also being conditioned. This conditioning usually has built-in punishments for "thinking for oneself" or other forms of "disloyalty." One way to break through this "catch 22" is to consider the effectiveness of extreme cases of control strategy—the "control freaks" and the tyrants. At first glance the tactics employed by these types may seem effective in controlling other people's behavior. However, if like me you have worked with such a person, you know that there are many tactics to counter a tyrannical boss—passive resistance, sabotage, and the channeling of huge amounts of time and energy into avoiding punishment, otherwise known as "covering your ass." In fact CYA accounts for a huge proportion of the efficiency losses in most workplaces, while the resulting bad morale and absenteeism due to stress-related illnesses eat up another big chunk.

Actually all behaviors motivated by fear are largely counter-productive to what we really want to achieve. Surely it's time to accept the fact that control, in any form, is not really an effective way to exercise power.

Nevertheless most organizations and institutions today are still organized around control strategies. They are hierarchical, elitist, and structured to reflect lines of command. Status and respect are conferred according to the height of one's position in the hierarchy, and information is provided on a need-to-know basis. Such a structure was presumably well suited to the Roman army after which it is modeled and may be suited to today's military operations. The structure was originally designed for winning in a game of life and death, where the front line participants were relatively uneducated. In any case they were expected to fight not to think. In most modern workplaces, however, workers tend to be highly skilled and to know more about their particular jobs than anyone else in the organization. That organizations of all types (from churches to businesses to governments) should still favor this command-and-control model is perhaps not surprising, even though it is ineffective today in most situations and quite unsuited to the expressed values, purpose, and talents of these organizations; it merely reflects how deep-seated the old assumptions about the nature of power are.

Another popular method of trying to control someone else's behavior is to urge them to change. The proponents of this approach usually believe that they are doing the other person a favor by pushing them to change for the better. Whether it is done by criticizing or as suggestions for improvement, this strategy almost always ends up being ineffective. The reason is that, regardless of how it is couched, *being urged to change is received as lack of acceptance.* How do you react when you are not accepted, you are criticized, or your weaknesses are being exposed? Doesn't your ego respond as it would to an attack?

This defensiveness is a natural, automatic reaction. Thus instead of facilitating the desired change or improvement in behavior, *criticism and its various facsimiles usually only serve to entrench the undesirable behavior.*

This conclusion deserves to be stressed because it is so contrary to the assumptions behind many parenting and managing techniques. It doesn't matter that some performance reviews involve mentioning positive feedback first or that parents mix praise and criticism. Everyone knows the "but" is coming; that's what they're waiting for, and that's what they'll react to. It doesn't matter whether we call them weaknesses or performance gaps, strategies that focus on eliminating or repairing faults will never be as effective as strategies that identify and build on strengths.

✴ An Opportunity for Personal Reflection ✴

How do you react to attempts to change, control, or manipulate you? What methods do you favor in trying to control others (children, employees, etc.)—carrot, stick, or a combination? Think of some examples of how you have used each method.

The Bulldozer Strategy

Subtlety is definitely not an aspect of this strategy for exercising power. Instead this strategy relies on the application of brute force to accomplish all its goals, even when less drastic measures are readily available. This strategy is exemplified by the manager (or parent) who yells, swears, pounds the table, or fires people for minor mistakes. I once worked with such a person. He was subject to frequent temper tantrums and once fired an employee who parked in the wrong spot. Minor conflicts were treated like major battles, with all the available firepower brought to bear. Respect for the environment or for people who might be hurt in this show of power was completely absent. His strategy may have bought him fearful submission, but it was bought at the cost of loyalty, respect, and genuine cooperation.

This application of extreme force is sometimes justified with the claim that less overall damage is done because the problem is resolved quickly and that "people who can't stand heat are quickly forced out of the kitchen." What force actually accomplishes, at best, is to make the symptoms of the problem disappear. The problem, however, has not gone away and may even have been exacerbated. The use of force as a strategy is especially dangerous when it is applied in conjunction with the control strategy discussed above. Here compliance is gained through the use of force in the form of threats and intimidation.

Because the use of force to solve problems or to get our own way is such a common strategy, we have all been on the receiving end of it at some time or other. Chances are we have also used it ourselves. I ask you now to consider as honestly as you can:

> "Does it work?"
>
> "Is fearful submission an effective way to achieve what you really want?"
>
> "Does the abusive man get a loving wife?"
>
> "Does the coercive boss get a loyal, dedicated employee?"

I think not.

The use of force may appear on the surface, or in the short run, to accomplish something. Actually, however, it usually serves to make people less motivated and to escalate conflicts. In so doing it obscures potentially creative, mutually acceptable solutions and opportunities for collaboration. Furthermore, the greater the force applied, the greater the resistance that will be encountered; thus, force ends up being counterproductive.

With enough force you may kill or destroy physical things, but *force is powerless against ideas, ideals, and ideologies*. Because it tends to create martyrs, the use of forceful measures often gives more power to an ideology than it had to start with. Surely we can conclude that *any strategy that uses fear as a motivator is a strategy of desperation and, as such, it cannot be considered an exercise of power.*

The Strategy of One-Upmanship

The strategy of "one-upmanship" is more of a finesse strategy than the other two. Its basis is the assumption that power is associated with status of some sort. If you outrank your competitor you have power over him. Others will bow to your superiority, accept your opinion without argument, and do your bidding. This superiority is sometimes based on something formal, such as position or title. My father, for example, lorded his doctorate over everyone, even in situations where a Ph.D. in chemistry was completely irrelevant. In other cases the superiority comes from some more subtle advantage such as height, possession of critical information, or facility with words.

Many times I have witnessed meetings and social gatherings being "high jacked" by an individual who manages to draw all the attention to himself or herself. At the beginning of the meeting many or all participants may engage in the game of one-upmanship, but usually it comes down to one or two individuals, and the others become reluctant spectators.

Commonly used tools for this strategy include: eliciting pity; using wit, put downs, or jargon; showing off; quoting from the policy manual; monopolizing the conversation; or speaking more loudly or more eloquently than anyone else. These same tools are used within families. A father of my acquaintance, for example, suddenly develops a very bad back to recapture attention from the family member in crisis. Children are especially good at the game of one-upmanship. If none of the usual tools work, a child may resort to bad behavior to draw attention.

In view of the emphasis in our society on competitiveness, it is not surprising that the strategy of one-upmanship is behind so many of our practices and institutions. Debate, for example, is a formalized way of playing the one-upmanship game. A less structured version is called discussion. Neither of these games is really about hearing another's point of view or learning anything new—it's about scoring points! This is perhaps most easily recognized in political debates, but I suggest it holds true for most discussions whether business meetings, union-management negotiations, family arguments, or religious discussions. This may be why people so often end up frustrated by meetings— they consume a lot of time and don't seem to accomplish much, especially not anything of a creative nature.

Many of the tools used in the game of one-upmanship have the function of *excluding* those who might threaten somebody's position of superiority. Jargon is a typical example. Jargon is a special language that is intelligible to a select few and is used to exclude all others from participating in the conversation or activity. Specialized knowledge, "in jokes," credentials, and dress codes all serve to maintain the special status of some by excluding others.

Using the strategies of one-upmanship you try to make yourself right by making someone else wrong, to make yourself rich by making someone else poor, to make yourself look good by making someone else look bad, i.e., you try to make yourself more powerful by making someone else less powerful. The product of these strategies is opposition, not cooperation, and resentment, rather than endorsement. Clearly these strategies are incapable of supporting real or lasting power.

If business meetings are ineffective, negotiations too protracted, politics too partisan, communication too unidirectional, or relationships somewhat dysfunctional, maybe it's time we looked at the effectiveness of the strategies being employed and the underlying motives of the participants. In my experience meetings can be effective and creative, partisanship has occasionally been set aside in the interest of the common good, people can have meaningful dialogue, negotiations can be non-confrontational, and relationships can be more functional. For example, in times of great crisis, people often respond with acts of selfless courage and cooperation in aid of a common cause. These outcomes only happen however when the strategy of one-upmanship is temporarily suspended.

✳ *An Opportunity for Personal Reflection* ✳

What techniques do you use to maintain control?

If you are not getting your own way, what do you do to change that situation?

What do you do to get "one up" on your colleagues? your competitors? your kids? your neighbors?

How easy is it for you to stay "king of the castle?"

Summary

The most frequently employed strategies for the exercise of power in the prevailing paradigm all have one thing in common. They are all based on establishing and maintaining *power over* people, things and situations. The strategies themselves may emphasize the use of *control, force,* or *status,* but they are all aimed at the success of one person or group without regard for, or even at the expense of, others. The results of such strategies are often praised as being evidence of competitiveness, nationalism, a winning spirit, a self-made person, etc. A closer look at these strategies, however, suggests that although appearing to be successful, they may ultimately be producing many more losers than winners, causing increased stress and stress-related illness, wasting time, demotivating people, and decreasing creativity and productivity.

CHAPTER 8

Exercising Authentic Power through Self-Empowerment

As you let go of the old beliefs and related strategies that are keeping you powerless, your quest for authentic power will lead you back to your Self and the authentic power that lies buried within you. According to this new way of thinking about power, *nobody else can empower you, and the only person you can empower is yourself*. It's up to you to adopt the tactics that will help you to do the work of uncovering your innate power and accessing it so that you can exercise it effectively. There is no one procedure for doing this; the task is too personal for a universal prescription. For this reason I have set out some possibilities in this chapter and the next.

I urge you to experiment with these techniques and adapt them to suit your own unique preferences and the particular stage in the empowerment process you are in at the time. As you become your Self, you will empower yourself. On the other hand, when you react to life in fear, seeking security through control, force, or status, and hiding behind all the things that you are not, then you hold yourself back from experiencing the power of living authentically.

Accessing the Full Power of the Techniques

Undoubtedly many, if not all, of the strategies and techniques for exercising authentic power that I present here will not be new to you. After all, I didn't invent them. I describe them briefly only for the purpose of providing *examples* of how authentic power *might* play out in the workplace specifically and in interpersonal relationships generally.

It is important to understand, however, that *the use of these techniques is not a recipe for authentic power.* The real power of these strategies and techniques originates *inside you*—from the motivation and attitude that you bring to them—not from the techniques themselves. In his books, Steven Covey refers, to "principle-centered leadership" and "principle-centered living" for the same reason. Research by Frederick Reichheld, reported in the *Harvard Business Review* (July–August 2001), showed that "outstanding [employee] loyalty is the direct result of the words and deeds—the decisions and practices—of committed top executives *who have personal integrity*" (emphasis mine). The same would hold true for the relationship between parents and children or any other relationship-dependent endeavor. In other words *it's the principle or motivation behind the action that is responsible for its power, not the action itself.*

Any technique you use because it happens to be in fashion, to get someone "off your back," or because you just want a quick fix for a problem situation will not be effective. Often in fact, actions based on such motivations make matters worse because they are seen for what they really are—new ways to manipulate and control. For example, it's more demoralizing when a manager ignores or countermands the work of a committee he has appointed than if he had simply made the decision himself in the first place. It would similarly be counterproductive to form the committee according to people's places in the hierarchical structure instead of basing appointments on knowledge of the task and the ability to contribute.

Indeed any approach, if motivated by the belief system of the old paradigm, can only produce the same old ineffective result. It's the intention that determines the power, and the intention in this instance has not changed. *The secret of success lies not in the technique or action itself, but in the intention/motivation with which it is applied.*

Turn Off Your Autopilot More Often

When your life is on "auto pilot" you react to each situation as it develops in a predetermined, automatic way. You don't have to invest any conscious thought in the process—you just react. What allows you to live in this unconscious manner is a set of subconscious assumptions, beliefs, mental models, and paradigms that I refer to as your *ego*. Many of these beliefs, if you examined them consciously, would prove to be invalid. This is not so surprising if you consider that some were adopted as is from others (parents, teachers, friends, etc.). As a child you drew inferences from your experiences based on very limited perceptions. These also became incorporated into your belief system. If beliefs and assumptions are limiting your power, the first step in empowering yourself is to find ways to free your life from control by those beliefs.

When you are operating on autopilot, only the preprogrammed or default way of reacting presents itself so you appear not to have any choice. Taking manual (conscious) control of your life opens myriad new, otherwise unavailable possibilities.

✳ An Opportunity for Personal Reflection ✳

What is your automatic, habitual reaction:

- *When someone criticizes you?*
- *When someone insults you?*
- *When someone threatens you?*
- *When someone hits you?*
- *When someone crosses you up?*
- *When someone hurts you?*

Is it perhaps to give as good as you got (an eye for an eye and a tooth for a tooth) or is it maybe to withdraw, engage in self-pity, and "bad mouth" the other person?

If you now take the time to think about each of these situations, can you come up with alternative responses based perhaps on different assumptions about what is going on and why the other persons might have behaved the way they did?

The likelihood is that your automatic reaction to each of the above situations was affected, at least in part, by the assumption that those insults, criticisms, etc. were *directed at you*—in other words, you took them *personally*. But you could choose to put a different spin on what was happening. For example, given how your ego causes you to react automatically and without thinking, isn't it reasonable to assume that something similar was operating to cause the other person to be critical, to be insulting, to strike out, etc.? If so then it wasn't personal in the sense that anyone who happened to be in your place at that time would likely have received the same treatment. In any case it was not anything you did *per se* that caused their reaction, it was *how they perceived and interpreted your actions*—it was a function of their own set of beliefs and assumptions. In other words your automatic reaction and the other person's just happened to intersect. For all you know the other person might just be reacting to having had a "bad hair day!"

Suspending your automatic reaction long enough to explore other ways of thinking about the situation is what I call "turning off your autopilot." It is self-empowering in several respects. It short circuits your automatic reaction, thereby preventing you from unwittingly escalating the situation. It also keeps you from getting caught up in the other person's dramas, which, in turn, leaves you free to respond more constructively and creatively to their behavior. Furthermore with control by your ego switched off, the wisdom of your authentic Self becomes available and can provide you with powerful alternative ways to respond to the situation at hand.

Mindfulness

The degree of *mindfulness* and *focus* required to "operate on manual" also fosters empowerment because the selected goal is pursued with increased efficiency and effectiveness. When the mind is highly focused it is less likely to be distracted with judgmental thoughts. Similarly it is less likely to wander off to past or future concerns—it stays rooted in the *present moment*, which is the only place life really happens and, therefore, the only place real power can be exercised. You have probably discovered for yourself that attempts to do simultaneous multi-tasking usually result in each task taking longer than normal and being performed poorly at that. For multi-tasking to succeed, tasks need to be performed sequentially, with full attention to each separate task.

The power of single-minded, conscious attention is especially noticeable in interactions between people. Have you noticed that your mind is elsewhere while you are supposedly having a meeting or conversation with someone? Unfortunately it happens to all of us far too often. The next time you are going to converse with someone, try giving him or her your complete, undivided attention—even maintain eye contact throughout the conversation. If this approach is motivated by a genuine interest in the other person and what they have to say, that person will feel so wonderful about the meeting that he or she will want to support you and help to make good things happen for you. If, on the other hand, you are motivated by a desire to manipulate the other person—if this is just another gimmick you are using to control someone—then you might be better off thinking about what you are going to do after the meeting is over!

Maintaining a single-minded focus (autopilot turned off) is admittedly difficult to achieve for any length of time. The automatic reaction usually jumps into play pretty quickly, so this new tactic will require practice. You might try cultivating the habit of inserting a time delay (such as counting to ten) before allowing the autopilot to assume control. Even to stop in the middle of an automatic reaction, choose a more appropriate response, and change directions is often better than to be a robot controlled by your ego. Furthermore every time you countermand your ego, the easier it will be the next time. Eventually your automatic response will be more consistent with your authentic Self.

Harness the Power of Your Words

Words might well be the most powerful tool in our tactical toolbox. Like all power tools, however, they can be dangerous if not used carefully and thoughtfully. Words have the power to inspire, but they also have the power to destroy, to dishearten, and to undermine. Perhaps because we don't realize just how powerful words can be, we often use our words in self-destructive and self-defeating ways.

I sometimes use a simple muscle testing technique to demonstrate to my clients how powerful an effect the words one chooses can have on one's own body. You might like to try this procedure with a friend or colleague. I suggest you take turns being the tester and the subject. The first step is to get a feel for how much energy is required for the subject to hold his or her arm parallel to the floor, straight out from the shoulder, and be able to withstand firm but gentle pushes downward on the wrist administered by the tester. The subject, throughout all testing, should apply exactly this same minimum energy to hold the arm up and allow the arm to fall if that amount at any time becomes insufficient. The tester always uses the same downward force when testing muscle strength.

When tester and subject believe they are sufficiently "calibrated," the subject is asked (while holding the arm extended) to recall silently a time when he or she felt like a complete failure. The event should be recalled with as much sensory detail as possible. When the subject indicates that he or she is reliving that particular occasion, he or she is asked to say out loud "I am such a failure"; at that moment the tester applies the usual downward push on the subject's wrist.

Usually the subject's arm goes down easily, but when that doesn't happen the subject often admits to having used extra force to maintain the arm in its horizontal position. After shaking out his arm, the test is repeated—this time having the subject recall a specific occasion when he or she felt especially resourceful and successful. As the subject makes a statement about feeling resourceful, the arm strength is again tested. The usual result is that the arm has returned to its former strength or even tests stronger than normal If the muscles are so affected by saying the word "failure" to oneself, what do you think happens to all the other body organs? What do you suppose is the overall effect of the other words you say to yourself?

The power of words may really be a subset of the power of images because words tend to get converted into images in our minds. The image, together with its associated sensory properties, functions like a blueprint for the reality that the mind/body will do its best to create for us. In other words the images that our words create are treated by our minds as if they were real. This is why your mouth puckers up and saliva starts to flow when you form the image of squeezing lemon juice into your mouth. It is why your muscles get weaker when you talk of being a failure, and it is why any clearly imagined intention is so powerful. It is also why some of our self-talk is so limiting. The little statements that we make under our breath, "I'll never be able to _____," "What a klutz I am," "Nobody could ever love me," are taken at face value by our subconscious minds and acted on as such.

Talk about What You Want to Happen

Even if we tell ourselves what we *don't* want to happen, our mind still converts the undesired consequence into an image, and it is this image that it tries to manifest. If we tell ourselves, for example, that we don't want to mispronounce a word in a certain way, we are greatly increasing the chance of that very mistake occurring. This is why telling a child *not* to do a particular thing is as good as inviting them to do it. The same principle applies to adults. The elevator at a company where I was once employed had a sign in it telling passengers not to panic in the case of an elevator failure. What the sign actually did was to raise the anxiety level of everyone who read it.

In order to exercise the power of the mind effectively, *we need to tell ourselves and others what we want to have happen* instead of what we don't want to happen. Since most of us have been raised on "don'ts," our "default thought" is about what we don't want. Part of exercising authentic power, therefore, is to consciously choose a different way of talking to ourselves and to others. We need to be much more careful with the words we use, whether on signs, letters, or just casual talk. If the person making the sign in the elevator had known the importance of his choice of words, he might have written "stay calm." If a golfer knows how powerful words and images are, he or she will concentrate on where exactly the ball *should* land and not give any thought to undesirable possibilities. Now that we realize the power of words to affect our outcomes, let us use words with all the care that we would use any power tool. We can't do much about the words that others say to us, but we can begin to pay more attention to the words we use.

Listen for the Quiet Voice

The voice of the authentic Self is much softer than that of the ego. In fact the ego is usually making so much noise and flooding us with so many thoughts that we seldom hear the quiet voice of the authentic Self or even have time to listen for it. It is as if the ego's technique for maintaining control of our lives is to keep us constantly bombarded with thoughts and images. Just like a radio or TV station, "dead air time" is disallowed. As a society we are also uncomfortable with silence, so much so that one minute of silence on Remembrance Days seem like an eternity to some. Having grown up in an atmosphere of constant stimulation, we have no appreciation of silence or stillness.

If we are to exercise authentic power, however, we will first need to learn to gain access to the authentic Self, and that will involve making time and space for listening for the quiet voice inside us. It will mean being still and quieting the constant chatter of the mind. Whether you do this by some form of meditation and/or breathing exercises and/or being close to nature and/or some other technique is up to you. Whether the authentic Self presents itself in the form of intuition, wisdom, the voice of God, or some other way is not important. What is important is that you regularly practice techniques that help you to connect with that source of wisdom and power that I call the authentic Self.

Another kind of practice or discipline that can be used to strengthen the connection to your authentic Self is to *purposely* engage in thoughts and activities from which your ego is excluded. Gratitude and forgiveness, for example, could never come from the ego. This focus on *giving without condition, criteria, or cost* is the way of the authentic Self. The way of the ego is to focus on what will be gained.

Regardless of the techniques you use, accessing the authentic Self is really a matter of *quieting the mind*. The authentic Self is there all the time, waiting for your consciousness to apprehend it, waiting to provide you with all the wisdom and the power you need to live a life of purpose, fulfillment, and joy. Part of being able to hear the quiet voice is listening with the *expectation* that it *is* there and that it is trying to communicate with you.

An Ounce of Intention Is Better than a Pound of Perspiration

This strategy for empowering yourself can be summed up by that old cliché, "Work smarter not harder." This is generally more difficult than it sounds because our society is very action-oriented. This preoccupation with doing something allows us to skip over the critical questions, *what?* and *why?* These are the empowering questions because they cause us to focus on our goal and to question our motivation. Are we doing this task because it's what is expected or are we acting on our values? Are we giving in to expediency or are we creating something of meaning?

If you take the time first to consciously clarify the goal and motivation for an intention, you will find that the conversion of that intention into reality requires much less effort than you are accustomed to exerting. A thought, in the form of an intention, is powerful in its own right; consequently, it requires much less effort to realize one's goal when it is associated with a strong, clear intention. Putting the emphasis on action, as most of us are accustomed to doing, ends up being harder work for a less satisfying result.

Asking the *What* and *Why* Questions

It is important for self-empowerment using this strategy to ask ourselves the what and why questions *before* investing ourselves in action:

> "What is my final destination?" or "Where will I be when I get where I'm going?"
>
> "Why do I intend to go there?"

The answers to these fundamental questions will guide your life and help you to create your own destiny because these questions are asking you to be clear about your intentions. They could be asked about your life, generally, in which case they would be probing your sense of your unique purpose in life. Or they could equally be asked about whatever you are involved in right now. They're asking you to be honest with yourself about why you are doing what you're doing and what your ultimate objective is.

At first glance these might seem like fairly easy questions to answer. For many of the people to whom I've talked, however, they are not easy; these people have apparently set out on a journey without being really clear about their destination. As the saying from *Alice in Wonderland* goes "If you don't know where you want to go, then any road will do." You would never know from observing them, however, that these people have little or no idea of their destination; these tend to be very busy people—too busy, they say, to do the things that are really important to them. Even though they don't know where they are going, they seem to be in an awful hurry to get there! Similarly many companies and organizations devote untold resources to strategic planning before they have agreed on a clear vision of where they want to go and what they want it to look like when they get there.

What are these people so busy doing in all their frantic busyness? They're *reacting* to the circumstances that life presents them with; they're busy coping, solving problems, making a living, and at the same time trying to get their own needs met. Clearly this is not a way to express authentic power! When people are expressing authentic power they are *creating their own destiny*.

Creating Your Own Destiny

Creating your own destiny is a quite different process than reacting as best you can to whatever comes along or solving problems; it requires a shift in how you see yourself. You need to move from seeing yourself (or your company's performance) as constrained by circumstances to a belief in your inherent ability to create the results you choose. Only as you embrace this belief will you begin to experience its power.

When you focus on problems, problems are what you tend to perpetuate. If, for example, you are focused on a problem such as being overweight, then obesity is the reality that you will likely keep creating. The harder you focus on the problem, the more likely the problem is to keep reappearing. Similarly if you are preoccupied with all the barriers between you and your goal, then barriers will be your experience of life. On the other hand, if you focus your intention on what you want to create and why you want to create it (i.e., where you will be when you get where you are going and what was the reason for undertaking the journey in the first place), then your chances of achieving that outcome will be greatly enhanced.

One way of explaining why visioning is a more effective approach than problem-solving is to contrast how the momentum changes over time in each case. As we succeed in making progress *toward* our vision, motivation and momentum will *increase*; whereas, as we succeed in solving a problem (i.e., moving *away* from it), our degree of motivation will *decrease*, and efforts will lessen until eventually the problem begins to reappear.

In order to apply visioning as a tactic for creating our destiny, there are some important aspects of the process of which you should be aware. Notice, for example, that the emphasis is on the destination as opposed to *how* you are going to get there or some intermediate stop along the way. Frequently these get confused in our minds. When this happens, the method loses its power. When asked about his goals, someone might say, "I want to have financial security." If I then ask him what he will do when he has financial security, he might say, "I'll retire." In other words financial security was not the outcome he wanted; it was merely a means to that end. If again asked, "Why do you want to retire?" he might reply that he would really like to travel and see the world. Obviously retirement was not the desired outcome either; it was travel. Retirement was just another *how to* on the way to getting where this person wanted to go. By assuming that the best way to be able to travel was to become financially secure and then retire, this person would exclude many other possibilities (such as being paid to travel as part of the job).

One further example will illustrate why focusing on the path is not as self-empowering as focusing on the final destination. A young woman in one of my groups listed "appropriate weight" as her goal. On further questioning she disclosed that she wanted to be thinner in order to be more attractive to men, and she saw the weight loss as a necessary means to that end. It turned out that what she really wanted was to create a relationship where she could be truly loved for who she was. Can you see that the tactic that she was pursuing was not likely to get her this result? Quite the opposite, it was likely to find a man who was attracted by thinness, not by who she really was inside that "right-sized" body. By focusing on the final destination you will not only leave yourself open to other potentially better ways to get to that destination, but also increase the likelihood that you will feel satisfied when you arrive.

Your intention should ideally be imagined, using as many sensory inputs as possible. It should be imagined in the present tense, *i.e.*, as if you had already achieved it. Such a clearly envisioned intention is indeed a very powerful tool. Be careful, therefore, that this outcome is what you truly want. Otherwise you run the risk of realizing too late that it is only what you thought you *should* want, based on the opinions of others or some whim of your ego.

Maximize Possibilities

Another approach to self-empowerment is to keep as many "doors open" as possible. Most of us are accustomed to thinking that maximizing possibilities involves being actively "in control." Especially if we have done the work of establishing a strong intention/goal/ vision, we think we need to protect it, keep it on course, give it the occasional strong push and eliminate any potential threats, somewhat like an over-protective parent. What that approach actually does is limit possibilities.

When we select one path and insist on following it, we are excluding the myriad other possible ways of reaching the same goal. Often other, better paths go unnoticed because we are so absorbed in controlling our progress along the chosen one. In contrast, the ability to *relinquish control* and to *trust* the power of intentions is the way to authentic power.

I use the model of an open hand to remind me to *trust the process*. (According to your preference, you might instead refer to trusting God or trusting the creative power of the universe). I picture my intention, clearly envisioned and aligned with my authentic Self, supported in the palm of my open hand. I remind myself that if I try to *control* the progress of my intention in any way, no matter how well meant the action might be, it will be equivalent to closing my fingers around my intention and smothering it—cutting it off from the countless possibilities that would otherwise be available to it. Those possibilities are only accessible to those able to keep the hand open and to trust.

In this model the intention, is not formed and then abandoned; it is supported by the open hand, but given the freedom to develop unhindered. To relinquish control and trust in this way requires courage, to be sure. Parents and leaders of all types who have employed this approach, however, will attest to its power.

One of my students coined the term *flexible contentment* to express what practicing trust was like for her. *Flexible* reminds me of the openness of the open hand—being open to the infinite number of possibilities that are part of authentic power. Flexible also reminds me of *surrender*. Unfortunately surrender has connotations of losing in the old win-lose definition of power. To the authentic Self, however, it means to bend as the tree bends in the wind without breaking—to give up futile resistance and instead to *be attentive for the presence of possibility in every situation*. It suggests that with trust and acceptance come that much-sought-after condition we call "peace of mind."

Give Wisdom a Chance

We are accustomed to thinking in terms of knowledge, not wisdom—"knowledge is power," or so we say. This may be true in the sense that knowledge, know-how, and information are all valuable tools. Like all tools they can be used constructively or destructively. Unfortunately knowledge and its various facsimiles are often used to maintain power over people and things, i.e., to manipulate, control and exploit.

Information comes from outside of us; it has to be acquired. Information has value; it can be purchased. When information accumulates in an individual, it becomes knowledge. Knowledge is a valued *possession* in our culture. As such it has become one more basis for elitism.

Not to possess knowledge usually means that you will be exploited and or marginalized in our society—the young, the old, the poor, and the learning-challenged. No wonder that students whose grades are below average are quickly identified as losers. No wonder the success of our education system is measured in terms of its ability to cram facts, theories, and skills into people so that they can be regurgitated in some standardized test format. The motivation of these students is often fear of failure, the need for validation by others, or the desire to beat someone else. Knowledge acquired in this way and used for these purposes is surely not an exercise of true power.

Wisdom Is More Powerful than Knowledge

We live in the so-called "information age." Information in a variety of formats is more easily available than at any other time in history. Yet paradoxically, the more we know, the less we seem to understand. No amount of knowledge, even in the hands of smart people, is sufficient to create the understanding, self-awareness, and meaning that are part of wisdom. Without understanding we have no ability to integrate the great abundance of information and knowledge we have acquired into a meaningful and interconnected whole. If we can't make sense of it, it provides us with little real power; instead we end up, both individually and organizationally, stuck in "information overload."

Without wisdom to show us the connections between things, the specialized knowledge we bring to bear in solving one problem ends up causing problems elsewhere in our lives or in our organizations. The money we think we are saving by consulting expert knowledge in one area very often turns out to be money wasted because the systemic roots of the problem were not understood and therefore not addressed. For example a program to cut costs in a corporation can result in less money for training, quality assurance, and safety concerns, as well as a greater workload for those remaining after the cut backs. Employees are likely to have lower morale, more stress, confusion, and frustration, and require more time off due to stress-related illness. Efficiency, productivity, and quality all suffer as a result; eventually so do sales—time to call in an expert in boosting sales! Yet, "in all cultures the wise person is the one who is able to make the right decision in circumstances in which reason [or knowledge] . . . [are] inadequate," says John Dalla Costa in his book, *Working Wisdom*. This is why he predicts that, "We are moving into an economic order in which wisdom, not labor or raw materials or capital, will become the key resource."

Wisdom is not a product of intellectual activity; this is why it is undervalued by most of our contemporaries. On the other hand much of the knowledge, facts, and truth that is valued in the conventional way of viewing power might more accurately be described as prejudice. This is because it is based on extremely limited perceptions. Perceptions change with time and from person-to-person. It's not that so-called facts are unimportant; it's just that they are far more powerful when used in conjunction with the wisdom of the authentic Self.

Cultivating Wisdom

The real power of knowledge only emerges through reflection as it is combined with meaning, experience, values, and intuition to form understanding, self-awareness, and, eventually, wisdom. This means that wisdom is the product of a raised consciousness. *With consciousness, every experience provides opportunities for insight, self-knowledge, and self-empowerment.* In contrast to knowledge, wisdom is not something you can buy or acquire from someone else. Wisdom derives from within—from the authentic Self. Children often display more wisdom than adults because they are still authentic—they have not yet been brainwashed.

If wisdom is to have a chance to be part of our new power base, we will also have to learn to put it to use and trust in its power. This means, among other things, not having to have scientific proof for everything. It means relying on your own wisdom or intuition to guide you. It means seeking out and valuing the wisdom that each person has to contribute regardless of their status in society. It means more emphasis on "heart" (the quiet voice) and less on "head" (the noisy mind). It means taking the time for reflection and meditation.

Summary

What is important in considering the exercise of authentic power is not the action or technique *per se*, but the intention (i.e., goal and motivation) behind the action. Although many of the suggested techniques may be familiar to you, their effectiveness will depend on your ability to apply them with a new motivation based on a new set of beliefs about the nature of power.

Authentic power originates inside you. No one else can empower you—you will have to do that for yourself. Therefore the exercise of authentic power is, first and foremost, a matter of self-empowerment. There is no single right path to self-empowerment. The suggested strategies and techniques should be considered as examples only.

Self-empowerment requires that your actions be motivated by your authentic Self, which in turn requires that you begin to free yourself from control by the preprogrammed beliefs that constitute your autopilot. It also requires you to pay more attention to the quiet voice of your authentic Self. Being extra careful with the words you use will keep you from inadvertently creating a self-fulfilling prophesy of the kind you don't want. On the other hand, forming a clear vision of where you'll be when you get where you're going and precisely why you want to go there will help you to turn your intentions into the right kind of self-fulfilling prophesies.

For those intentions to realize their full power, however, it is important to resist your urge to control everything and to allow yourself to trust the process. Your self-empowerment will also be enhanced if you take time for the reflection necessary to achieve the understanding, sense of meaning, and self-awareness that are part of wisdom.

CHAPTER 9

Creating an Environment for Self-Empowerment

I t is true that no one else can empower you—not me, not your boss, not your parents or your spouse. What others can do for you and you for others is to *create an environment* that fosters the process of self-empowerment as described in the previous chapter. You can also create an appropriate environment for your own empowerment. This is an important strategy in the exercise of authentic power because authentic power is based on having *power with* others. If we're all in this together, then creating an environment in which we can all be successful in our attempts at self-empowerment would seem to be a good strategy.

Great leaders create environments in which people's abilities emerge and develop naturally in the course of doing whatever it is that they are doing. The ability to create a self-empowering environment comes from having made the shift from the beliefs of the prevailing paradigm to a belief in the inherent greatness in all people. Note that I use the word *create* to describe this strategy. This term is meant to imply the conscious choice of an intention motivated by your authentic Self. The word *environment* is also significant in that it denotes the need to work on many different fronts to advance this strategy; it will not be sufficient to focus on only a single aspect of the overall environment. Bearing this in mind I have presented below a few of the many tactics you might employ to help create this kind of environment.

Follow the Lesson of the Dresser Drawer

In our summer cottage is a dresser drawer that holds a profound lesson for anyone wanting to create an environment for empowerment. If you ever tried to push in that drawer after it had been pulled out, you would probably choose other words to describe it—some of which would undoubtedly not bear repeating. The reason is, quite frankly, that this drawer can be very frustrating. It apparently doesn't like to be pushed shut. The harder you push on it, the more it resists, until it finally can't be budged in either direction. This is the point at which my wife always yells for me to come and push in the "blankety-blank" drawer. In my hands, however, the drawer slides gently and smoothly into place. Needless to say, this does nothing to ease my wife's frustration.

Have you ever tried to change someone—an employee, a child or a spouse perhaps? Did you end up as frustrated as my wife does with that dresser drawer? Chances are you did. Actually Newton described this phenomenon many years ago with a law of physics that says, "The harder you push on something, the harder it pushes back." My point is that you can't change people simply by urging them to change. The more you push, the more resistant they will likely become, even if they themselves want to change.

Why, other than Newton's law about physical objects, should people be so contrary? I believe it is because they are hearing the suggestion to change as criticism of how they are. This is the natural reaction of the ego to any form of attack. Criticism is interpreted by the ego as a personal attack, and— your stated intention not withstanding—as an attempt to exert control. Immediately and automatically all the defenses of the ego are aroused. The defensive reaction may take the form of active aggression, accentuating the criticized behavior, arguing, shifting blame, or even passive withdrawal. What it will not likely do is facilitate the desired change!

What's my secret, then, for dealing with that drawer that reacts so strongly to being pushed in? Well, first I start by pulling it, very gently, a little further out. Then I guide it very slowly and gently into place. If at any time it resists going in, I again slide it out a little before resuming the smooth slide into place. The lesson of that dresser drawer is that *change begins with acceptance not force*. The drawer demonstrates that *force is counterproductive to change*.

The bulldozer strategy, based on force, is part of the old paradigm of power. The new, authentic paradigm replaces force and coercion with acceptance and respect. In gentle, respectful hands, the drawer glides easily into place. *In an environment of understanding, acceptance and encouragement, people are enabled to face the difficult, often painful task of change and growth that is an essential part of self-empowerment.* Acceptance does not mean accepting a person's behavior; it refers to how you relate to the person behind the behavior. As that true Self is recognized and shown acceptance, it will be able to assert itself over the ego, and then real change and empowerment can occur.

That dresser drawer has much to teach us about our relationships with others and how to enable them to grow and change. Even more valuable, perhaps, would be to apply the lesson of the drawer to ourselves—to learn that the loving *acceptance* of ourselves is the only environment in which meaningful growth will take place. So often my clients have been able to apply the lesson of the drawer in their relationships with others, but when it came to themselves, they were judgmental, critical, and demanding. The more so they were, the harder they found it to effect the desired changes in themselves and the more they reacted by beating up on themselves as failures. That approach doesn't work for the dresser drawer; neither does it create a self-empowering environment for people.

The surprising power of acceptance, it should be noted, comes only with a major paradigm shift—a shift of emphasis from *getting* understanding, forgiveness, or a sense of belonging to *giving* these things without condition, cost, or criteria. In terms of the corresponding vector diagram, it's a shift from an arrow pointing downward to one pointing upward. It's a 180 degree shift for most of us because we are so highly focused on being understood, forgiven, etc. For example we don't listen with an intention to understand; we listen so that we can make a rebuttal—so that we can be understood. When the problem remains unresolved, we conclude, "they just don't understand."

Use an Upside-Down Pyramid

Structure or form is most effective when it serves function. If our strategy is to create an environment that fosters and enables self-empowerment, we would do well to consider what kind of organizational structure might best serve that strategy. It is unlikely that a command and control structure would be suited to this approach. Instead the structure would need to emphasize the mentoring, coaching, and enabling roles of all managers and supervisors. In fact the people in these positions probably wouldn't be called managers or supervisors because these names suggest roles that would no longer be appropriate. *Leaders* would adapt their coaching style to fit each separate person in their care. Positions of leadership would not confer special status or prestige. Instead the value and unique gifts of each and every member of the organization would be recognized, appreciated, and maximized.

Does this lack of hierarchical status imply a non-pyramidal structure? I think not. The pyramid would, however, have a very different significance. It would arise naturally because each leader would have a practical limit of, say, eight-to-ten people who could adequately be cared for, mentored, and enabled. In turn, every eight-to-ten of these leaders would require a leader (mentor) of their own, and so on, creating another pyramid-shaped organization chart. Perhaps, to avoid confusing the resulting structure with a conventional power-based pyramid, the pyramid could be drawn upside-down, with the front-line workers at the top. This would remind everyone who saw it of the importance to the organization of supporting those people who are most closely in touch with the purpose for which the organization exists—the workers who produce the product or deliver the service.

The upside-down pyramid symbolizes a structural approach that is more than just a model for business organizations. Imagine how much more effective health care might be if every person in the system, including the patient, felt valued as an integral part of the team. A critical component in all types of healing is compassion. A health care system, therefore, that treats people like so many mechanical devices that need to be repaired and shipped out cannot be truly effective in fulfilling its purpose. The problem is not just that machines are increasingly replacing the need for human contact, the problem is also in the structure that so undervalues the role of those humans who do have contact with the patient. Consequently they feel pressured, unappreciated, and alienated. Health care workers cannot be expected to treat the patients any better than they themselves are treated.

The same could be said for workers in any field. The closer a worker is to the bottom of the conventional hierarchical pyramid, the more undervalued he or she is likely to feel. This feeling cannot help but be reflected in how these workers treat customers or other workers who are perceived to be even lower in the pecking order. Contrast this with the potential for effectiveness of organizations that are structured so that every member of the organization is valued and enabled to optimize their contribution to the organization's purpose.

Build on Rock, Not Sand

It's an old analogy—the advantages of building a house on rock versus sand—but it's also memorable, and so I'm hoping it will remind us to build our lives and our organizations around our strengths instead of our weaknesses. It may seem that this is too obvious a tactic to require a reminder. My observations, however, suggest that many of the environments in which we work, learn, and interact are not conducive to self-empowerment precisely because they are focused on correcting faults, improving areas of perceived weakness, and doing tasks that are outside the areas of our greatest strengths.

When we are placed in an environment in which we can excel, it's not only more enjoyable, it's also easier to become even better—to reach our true potential, to empower ourselves. In this instance the predominant image in our minds—the one that influences our emotional and behavioral response—is of success. On the other hand a major focus on improvement results in a mental image of weakness or failure or low value, which consequently becomes a self-fulfilling prophecy in the wrong direction. Furthermore it arouses the kinds of defensive behavior I described under the topic of "the dresser drawer."

This is why performance reviews that include "areas for improvement," are usually not effective in achieving the desired results. An environment that is more conducive to self-empowerment will be achieved when a person's unique strengths are identified and they are enabled to exercise these and build on them. The natural response to such an environment, as the person feels like a valuable contributor, is a desire to improve even further. This increasing understanding of and comfort with who they really are will enable these persons to concern themselves less and less with maintaining the false images that the ego promotes. This is part of the process of self-empowerment.

Build Synergy (*Power With*)

The only thing more powerful than the exercise of authentic power by an individual is a group of individuals exercising authentic power together. Tactics designed to promote this kind of cooperation will take into account the deep human need for *belonging*. This kind of belonging has nothing to do with ownership. It describes the *longing* that all of us have *to be*—to *be* accepted, to *be* connected to something more grand, to *be* "in communion" with others, to *be* valued.

Be a Catalyst

Most chemical reactions take place only when subjected to extremes of temperature, pressure, or concentration. As a result, chemical-based processes tend to be inefficient, slow, and wasteful (i.e., they generate a lot of unwanted by-products). In these respects they are analogous to tactics associated with the bulldozer approach. In contrast, the chemical reactions that take place inside living things (i.e., biochemical reactions), are highly specific (generate very few by-products), take place at body temperature and ambient pressures, and, as a result, are extremely efficient. The magic ingredients in biological systems are enzymes, which function as catalysts. The catalyst brings the participants in the reaction together in the most advantageous way and then moves on to do the same thing again and again.

Another name for a person who performs a catalytic role is *facilitator*. There are many ways to facilitate the kinds of interaction needed for synergy.

- The *communication catalyst* will be a good "active listener" and also ensure that information is freely available in a form that is understandable to each recipient.
- The *mediator catalyst* will help participants to resolve disputes and misunderstandings before their positions become more polarized and hardened.
- The *inspiration catalyst* combines the ability to enroll others in a shared vision and the ability to cheer the team on. Inspiration catalysts know that passion is contagious, so their passion is expressed liberally and frequently. Such people also know that *who they are makes a difference*, and so they consciously act as role models.

Facilitation skills can be learned. Like any other learned skill, they need to be practiced regularly if they are to produce the desired synergy. I mentioned the facilitation skills involving communication, mediation, and inspiration in particular because I noticed that when I have been called into organizations as a facilitator, those were the skills that I called upon most frequently and that had the biggest impact on synergy—both the synergy between the client organization and me, and among the members of the organization.

For example, in one professional service organization I found that the professionals were not able to communicate with the nonprofessional staff; both groups were at odds with each other and with management, and morale was deteriorating. I helped them to really listen to each other with the intent to understand the other's point of view. Next we worked on developing a common vision of how we all wanted the organization to be. The participants were surprised at how similar their ideals really were. Having agreement on the kind of organization and outcome they wanted to achieve added excitement and inspiration. As the participants were enabled to communicate their individual aspirations and concerns to each other, conflicts were more easily resolved by mutual understanding and agreement.

Work for Consensus

Consensus doesn't mean compromise; nor does it mean unanimity. Decisions made by consensus will result in a higher level of cooperation because the process helps people's differing viewpoints to *converge* without devaluing anyone's contribution or making anyone wrong. Decisions by majority rule, on the other hand, tend to polarize differing opinions, thereby creating winners and losers.

In reaching a consensus it is important that every member of the group feels that his or her point of view has been heard and considered. This is the process I used with the above mentioned group of professionals, staff, and management to arrive at agreement on a vision statement. The aim of the group was to pool their individual ideas to arrive at the best possible outcome, i.e., to achieve synergy. Often an idea that is not acceptable to the group is the starting point for a creative new idea. Having felt part of the group process, even if their idea is not the one chosen, most people will be willing to cooperate in implementing the decision. At least they will be unlikely to sabotage it. The power of synergy cannot be experienced if part of the team is sitting back on their oars because they were outvoted or because they feel they were not listened to.

Getting "on side" with the rest of the team is usually more of an emotional matter than a rational one, in my experience. This is why debating or arguing rarely promotes consensus. On the other hand I have personally found that even highly charged issues can be resolved by consensus if care is taken to acknowledge and accept people's emotional reaction or their attachment to certain approaches. In one organization that was split over a very controversial decision, I went so far as to ask each member, in the presence of all the others, to express freely only their emotional reaction to the situation. Comments from others were not permitted at that time. Once the emotional stuff was out of the way, the group was able to address the issues more calmly, and resolution quickly followed. The last time I checked this group was still working together in a spirit of cooperation and goodwill. Emotional reactions drain away the energy without which synergy is impossible; consensus allows the passion to be channeled toward a common goal instead of breaking the group apart.

Conspire to Cooperate

According to its Latin roots, to *conspire* simply means to "breathe together." Breathing in unison with another person is a technique that has been described by the hypnotherapist Milton Erickson as a way of establishing *rapport*. I am using conspire, therefore, as a figurative way of referring to any technique that builds rapport among the members of a group. You could also think of it as building "right relationships."

Relationships that foster cooperation and synergy cannot thrive in an atmosphere of competition, power struggles, greed, or fear. On the other hand when we relate to others as intrinsically worthy, wise, and wonderful human beings, we remove some of their need to grab success, affirmation, or status for themselves—there is plenty to go around. When people feel supported and not threatened by others, they can let down their guard and be themselves. Time and energy wasted on power struggles can be freed up in favor of creativity and cooperation. Sharing can replace greed and competition. These changes bring more authentic power to the whole group.

Rapport is best established in informal ways and settings; it can't be forced. You will need to make time to get to know your fellow team members. If you are a leader trying to develop the excellent performance that is associated with synergy, you may want to consciously provide opportunities for building rapport among the team members. You don't necessarily need a wilderness experience together or a course on ropes and ladders. You do need, however, to create an environment where it is safe for people to allow themselves to be vulnerable—where they can learn to accept and trust each other.

Scott Peck, author of *The Different Drum*, calls this process "community building." Community, according to *The Foundation For Community Encouragement, Inc.*, founded by Dr. Peck, is "a safe place to release protective identities and to create an environment where self-discovery and shared understanding can flourish." I have personally attended one of the community-building workshops organized by this foundation and can attest to the empowerment that took place among fifty strangers over the course of four days.

I have been most successful in developing that kind of rapport with other members of my team when I have been able to convincingly step outside my role as manager and just be "Ross." I recall one instance particularly when I participated in a role-playing exercise. Others mentioned afterwards that they had had no idea that I was affected by a particular issue the same way they were. This new understanding and shared burden brought us closer together than any written memo or inspirational talk to the staff had ever done.

Summary

You cannot empower another person—even if you want to. What you can do—indeed what you must do—if you are to exercise authentic power, is to *create an environment that fosters self-empowerment*. The environment that will enable others to become more powerful is the same environment that makes possible your own empowerment. This empowering environment features enhanced acceptance of others and yourself, organizational structures that are consistent with this objective, and practices that build on people's strengths. As others are enabled to become more genuinely powerful so will you and *vice versa*.

Authentic power can also be exercised using strategies to build synergy. Specific suggestions include facilitating communication, timely resolution of conflicts, inspiration of groups or teams, getting everyone on board by building consensus, and establishing rapport.

These are not new strategies or approaches. When used in the context of the new paradigm, however, they have proved effective ways of exercising authentic power.

More Power to You:
The Transition
to Authentic Power

E ven after you have learned how to recognize authentic power and to differentiate it from the prevailing notions of power—even after you have learned where to look for it, how it is exercised, and what limits your ability to access it—even then, the quest is not over. It is not sufficient to know what authentic power will look like when you find it, what to do with it when you find it, or even to have obtained the map showing its location. You still have to make the journey from where you are to where the elusive prize awaits you. This is no trivial task.

Letting go of the habits of a lifetime and the beliefs on which these habits are based is a slow and often painful process. The path is fraught with hazards—barriers to be surmounted and pitfalls to be avoided. You will need to be on guard because things are often not as they appear. What may look like a short-cut is probably a dead end; what appears to be a problem or a setback may contain the very opportunity you've been waiting for; and what claims to be real power may only be an alluring illusion. On the other hand, the ability to manifest in one's life the deepest desires of the heart is a prize worthy of such a quest.

Dismantling the Barriers

The main barrier to moving forward on the quest is your own system of beliefs that I have characterized as your ego. Once you realize this fact, however, the barrier doesn't seem as formidable. It's really like a house of cards in that the beliefs are held in place by yet another belief. This is the belief that someone or something else is preventing you from moving forward. Remove that one belief and the others collapse relatively easily. This is why I've done my best to help you get past these limitations by exposing as untrue your belief about what exactly is holding you back and making you feel powerless.

Once you have consciously recognized this barrier for what it is, you have a second barrier to deal with. This barrier is your set of habitual behaviors. Like all habits they are hard to break because they have been so firmly ingrained. Nevertheless, like other habits, with sufficient determination they can be broken. Because these habits are associated with your old belief system, as the beliefs are discarded in favor of new ones, it will be easier and easier to let go of old, ineffective behaviors.

Avoiding the Pitfalls

The main trick that the ego uses to keep you in its control and, therefore, unable to experience authentic power, is to keep introducing thoughts of doubt and fear:

"What if I don't succeed?"

"What will people think?"

"Will people think that I am weak; will they take advantage of me?"

"These ideas are so radical, can they really work?"

You will find that it doesn't take much to throw you off course and bring you back to the limiting beliefs and fears that have held you prisoner for so long. After a while it's easy to become discouraged and give up the quest because you have not succeeded in experiencing authentic power. The catch, however, is that it is impossible to access authentic power as long as you doubt either that you possess such a power or that you can use it to manifest in your life what is truly important to you.

It's not that authentic power is locked away in some hidden, far off place. You already have it in your possession, but your own ego keeps it hidden from you and does its best to convince you, not only that there is no such power, but also that people will ridicule you or take advantage of you if you fail to heed the advice of your ego. Thus the predominant motivation behind your choices to act or not to act continues to be ego-generated fear. The vector (arrow) representing these intentions is pointed in the opposite direction from intentions motivated by your authentic Self. As a result your quest will lead only to frustration, and after a while it's easy to become discouraged and abandon the quest entirely. Now that you know how to recognize this pitfall, however, you will be better able to avoid it.

You should also be aware of the possibility that your ego may try to hide its true agenda by couching its motives in terms that sound like they are coming from the authentic Self. The ego can be very persuasive. It can make you believe that you are choosing an action based on the best interests of others when it is really your own interests that are being served. For example, you may be convinced that your harsh criticism of another is for their own good—that you are only trying to make them a better person. In reality, however, it may be simply a way to make you feel superior, possibly to control the other person or to manipulate them into behaving as you wish they would. Judgmental criticism is not the way of the authentic Self, even if your ego makes it seem as if it is. You will need to be especially wary of this pitfall as you proceed on your quest for the experience of authentic power. Steering clear of this pitfall will require you to be really clear on all your intentions and to carefully examine the motivation behind each one to make certain that it is really what it purports to be.

If you do achieve some success in your quest for authentic power, your ego may employ yet another trick in order to reclaim your allegiance. The first taste of authentic power will probably be accompanied by increased status, recognition, and other image enhancements. At this point the danger of this last pitfall is at its highest. When caught up in the enjoyment of the rewards of success, you are more vulnerable than ever to being seduced by them. It's not that there is anything intrinsically wrong with recognition, fame, glory, etc. The danger is in becoming attached to or identifying with these things because it is as this happens that your newly discovered powers begin to wane.

As soon as you begin to sound like or act like an expert, a guru, or a god—BEWARE! When you identify more strongly with your image than with your authentic Self, your ego has managed to reassert itself. When you are more concerned about getting recognition and enhancing your image than you are about being true to your Self, then you have lost the connection to the Source of your power. This is why, for example, natural leaders in an organization sometimes cease to be as effective after their leadership has been recognized with a promotion to a position of higher status, or why political candidates, once elected, often seem to lose the very attributes that were responsible for their success.

This phenomenon in which something tends to happen to spoil our experience of power and authenticity just as it is beginning has given rise to several common expressions, "Power corrupts . . ." and "Pride goes before a fall." Perhaps, more in line with the metaphor I have used before that refers to the ego as *head* and the authentic Self as *heart*, are the expressions, "Don't let success go to your head." and "Don't get a swelled head." In acknowledging the role of the head (ego), these expressions warn us of a common pitfall in the quest for authentic power, namely the temptation to be distracted by the ego's preoccupation with fame and glory. The fact that the prevailing paradigm equates status with power makes this temptation especially hard to resist.

This is a trap that I fell into when I was being recruited to head up another, larger company. The more I hesitated, the more attractive the offers I received until I finally gave in to the temptation and accepted the position. I told myself that I was moving so that I could test my ideas about management in a different setting, but there was also the matter of increased status that I didn't completely acknowledge to myself. I will never know how much all the perquisites and status symbols that I had negotiated detracted from my ability to provide the kind of leadership in my new job that I exercised in my previous job and that had made me such a desirable recruit. I do know that I had to work extra hard to counteract the initial impression of me that these things created with the staff.

One final potential pitfall is the temptation to leap into action too quickly. You will be especially vulnerable to this danger if, like me, you have a cherished reputation as a problem-solver or doer. Busyness and hard work are highly regarded by our society, and so there is a natural tendency to skip over the important *what* and *why* questions and concern ourselves directly with the practicalities of *how* and *when*. We want to be seen to be doing something—anything. In our haste to get on with our quest for authentic power, however, we risk rushing off in the opposite direction. I am not advocating analysis paralysis. I am recommending that the appropriate action (if action is appropriate to the circumstance at hand) be allowed to develop out of a clearly thought out intention and motivation.

The urgency that we feel to do something often causes us to look to experts for direction and formulae. The quest for authentic power, however, is a creative process; each of us must discover our own answers to the *how* question. In his book *The Answer to How Is Yes* Peter Block expresses a similar thought:

> Whatever our destination, it is letting go of the practical imperative that is most likely to guide us to a larger sense of where we want to go and what values we want to embody in getting there. . . . What will matter most to us, upon deeper reflection, is the *quality* of experience we create in the world, not the *quantity* of the results. . . . When we follow fashion and ask for steps, recipes, and certainty, we deny our freedom, for we are trapped in the very act of asking the question. Following a recipe assumes that there is a known path and that someone else knows it. Our freedom asks us to follow an unknown path and to invent our own steps . . . —"to be the author of our own experience." (italics mine)

Getting Started

The quest for authentic power—though the path be unknown and though it be a journey of a thousand miles and take a lifetime to complete—still begins with the first step and proceeds with the next, and the next, and so on. You have already taken the first step by reading this book. You have been alerted to the awesome power hidden within you—the power to create your own destiny, to realize the deepest desires of your heart. You have been given some tools to aid you in your journey, warned of dangers you might encounter along the way, and told of signposts that will guide you. The lamp of wisdom, which is fueled by reflection, will light your way and help to dispel the darkness of unconsciousness. The pathway to authentic power stretches out before you. The next step is up to you.

Take heart—the journey is made up of more than just hazards and pitfalls! In addition to the ultimate goal, there are also many pleasant surprises to be enjoyed along the way. Unless you are still convinced that your old belief system is serving you well, I invite you to try out this new path. I'm confident that you will be happy you did. In any case *the journey is your life*, so you might as well create joy instead of suffering and disappointment. Frankly I think you will be surprised just how pleasant it is when you choose to live authentically. You might also consider the alternatives—if you are not living authentically, are you really living?

The Choice Is Yours

The *responsibility is yours* to choose between being a victim of fate, on the one hand, and exercising your power to create what your heart desires and to live your unique purpose, on the other hand. These choices are being made many times a day, probably many more times than you realize. Pause for a moment and think back over the last twenty-four hours. Think of all the choices you have made in that time period. Even when you do not act or react—that is also a choice. Even when you react automatically, without consciously pondering how you will react—that is your default *choice*.

Is your experience of life satisfying or frustrating?

Does it include the experience of authentic power or of powerlessness?

In any case, your experience is the net result of all those little choices—the ones you made consciously and the default choices, the ego-sponsored choices and the ones sponsored by your authentic Self.

Each and every choice you make, hundreds of them every day, represents an opportunity to contribute to the making of a stumbling block or a stepping stone in the quest for authentic power. Ego-motivated choices will produce stumbling blocks, whereas every time you make a choice that is true to your Self you are creating a stepping stone. Every choice motivated by respect—respect for other people, for yourself, and for the earth—will bring you one step closer to the realization of authentic power. Every choice made out of fear will take you in the direction of illusion and, ultimately, of disappointment.

On my bedroom wall when I was growing up hung a plaque with a message to remind me that in the final analysis, life will be whatever I make of it. Now the message hangs on the wall of my office. It is in front of me as I write this book. This is what it says:

> *Isn't it strange that Princes and Kings*
> *And Clowns that caper in Sawdust Rings*
> *And ordinary folk like you and me*
> *Are builders of eternity. . .*
>
> *To each is given a bag of tools*
> *An hour glass and a book of rules*
> *And each must build ere his time has flown*
> *A stumbling block or a stepping stone.*

(AUTHOR UNKNOWN)

BIBLIOGRAPHY

Block, Peter. *The Answer to How Is Yes: Acting on What Matters.* San Francisco: Berrett-Koehler, 2001.

Clifton, Donald O., and Paula Nelson. *Soar with Your Strengths.* New York: Dell, 1992.

Cohen, Kenneth S. 1999. "The Role of Intention in Cross-Cultural Healing Traditions." *Bridges: ISSEEM Magazine.* 10 no. 3: 8–11.

Covey, Stephen R. *Principle-Centered Leadership.* Fireside ed. New York. Simon & Schuster, 1991.

Dalla Costa, John. *Working Wisdom.* Toronto: Stoddart, 1995.

Dossey, Larry M.D. *Be Careful What You Pray For . . . You Just Might Get It: What We Can Do About the Unintentional Effects of Our Thoughts, Prayers, and Wishes.* New York: HarperSanFrancisco, 1997.

Dossey, Larry M.D. *Healing Words: The Power of Prayer and the Practice of Medicine.* New York: HarperSanFrancisco, 1993.

Eisler, Riane. *The Chalice and the Blade: Our History, Our Future.* Cambridge, MA: Harper & Row, 1987.

Eisler, Riane. *Sacred Pleasure. Sex, Myth, and the Politics of the Body.* New York: HarperSanFrancisco, 1995.

Gibran, Kahlil. *The Prophet.* New York: Alfred A. Knopf, 1923.

Kelly, Marjorie. *The Divine Right of Capital: Dethroning the Corporate Aristocracy.* San Francisco: Berrett-Koehler, 2001.

Kim, Daniel H. 1993. "Paradigm-Creating Loops: How Perceptions Shape Reality." *The Systems Thinker.* 4, no. 2: 1–3.

Machiavelli, Niccolo. *The Prince: A New Translation, Backgrounds, Interpretations.* Translated and edited by Robert M. Adams. A Norton Critical Edition. New York: W.W. Norton & Co., 1977.

Maslow, Abraham H. *Dominance, Self-Esteem, Self-Actualization: Germinal Papers of A. H. Maslow.* Edited by Richard J. Lowry. Monterey, CA.: Brooks/Cole Publishing Co., 1973.

Maslow, Abraham H. *The Farther Reaches of Human Nature.* New York: Viking Press, 1971.

Maslow, Abraham H. *Toward a Psychology of Being.* 2nd ed. New York: Van Nostrand Reinhold Co., 1968.

Orwell, George. *Nineteen Eighty-Four: A Novel.* London: Secker & Warburg, 1949.

Bibliography

Peck, Scott M. M.D. *The Different Drum: Community-Making and Peace.* A Touchstone Book. New York: Simon & Schuster, 1987.

Reichheld, Frederick F. 2001. "Lead for Loyalty." *Harvard Business Review.* (July-August): 76–84.

Senge, Peter M. *The Fifth Discipline: The Art and Practice of the Learning Organization.* A Currency Book. New York: Doubleday, 1990.

Tolle, Eckhart. *The Power of Now: A Guide to Spiritual Enlightenment.* Vancouver: Namaste Publishing, 1997.

Webster's New Explorer Dictionary: Created in Cooperation with the Editors of Merriam-Webster. Springfield, MA: Federal Street Press, 1999.

Wink, Walter. *Engaging the Powers: Discernment and Resistance in a World of Domination.* Minneapolis: Fortress Press, 1992.

INDEX

Index

Index

W

Weakness, 48
Weber, Andrew Lloyd, *Jesus Christ Superstar*, 11
Webster's New Explorer Dictionary, definition of power, 12
What questions, 108–110, 135
When questions, 135–136
Wholeness, 47
Why questions, 108–110, 135
Will power, 28
Win-lose, 59, 113
Win-win, 57

Wink, Walter, *Engaging the Powers*, 32
Winners, 57–59
Wisdom, 107, 113–116, 137
Wit, 95
Words
  love, 12
  power of, 104–107
  and the word *power*, 11–12
Working Wisdom (Costa), 115

Y

Yi, 64

ABOUT THE AUTHOR

G. ROSS LAWFORD brings to his writing his professional experience as a research scientist, university professor, business executive, wellness coach, facilitator, and consultant. Just as importantly, he incorporates into his writing reflections on his roles as son, parent, brother, spouse, friend, and volunteer leader in community organizations such as the board of the local hospital.

Ross followed his father's footsteps in earning a Ph.D. in biochemistry from the University of Toronto. He was a member of the Faculty of Health Sciences at McMaster University before assuming executive positions, first within a large manufacturing and retail conglomerate for sixteen years, and later in a smaller technical services firm. While discharging these responsibilities he focused his experimentation, observation, and learning skills on the subjects of leadership and human dynamics within organizations.

Building on his skills as a facilitator, mentor, and coach, Ross founded a consulting practice under the name *Ross Lawford and Associates* in 1993. Having supplemented these skills with additional training in mediation and a variety of therapeutic techniques, he works with individuals, groups, and corporations to help people in their quest for fuller, healthier, and more meaningful professional and personal lives.

Ross lives in Toronto, Canada, with his wife of thirty-five years. They have two adult children. Ross may be contacted at rlawford@attcanada.ca

Berrett-Koehler Publishers

B ERRETT-KOEHLER is an independent publisher of books, periodicals, and other publications at the leading edge of new thinking and innovative practice on work, business, management, leadership, stewardship, career development, human resources, entrepreneurship, and global sustainability.

Since the company's founding in 1992, we have been committed to supporting the movement toward a more enlightened world of work by publishing books, periodicals, and other publications that help us to integrate our values with our work and work lives, and to create more humane and effective organizations.

We have chosen to focus on the areas of work, business, and organizations, because these are central elements in many people's lives today. Furthermore, the work world is going through tumultuous changes, from the decline of job security to the rise of new structures for organizing people and work. We believe that change is needed at all levels— individual, organizational, community, and global—and our publications address each of these levels.

We seek to create new lenses for understanding organizations, to legitimize topics that people care deeply about but that current business orthodoxy censors or considers secondary to bottom-line concerns, and to uncover new meaning, means, and ends for our work and work lives.

See next page for other publications from Berrett-Koehler

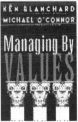

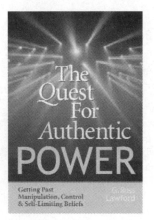